How to Master the IELTS

How to Master the IELTS

Over 400 practice questions for all parts
of the International English Language
Testing System

Chris Tyreman

KoganPage

LONDON PHILADELPHIA NEW DELHI

First published in Great Britain and the United States in 2012 by Kogan Page Limited

120 Pentonville Road	1518 Walnut Street, Suite 1100	4737/23 Ansari Road
London N1 9JN	Philadelphia PA 19102	Daryaganj
United Kingdom	USA	New Delhi 110002
www.koganpage.com		India

© Chris Tyreman, 2012

ISBN   978 0 7494 5636 8
E-ISBN   978 0 7494 5946 8

British Library Cataloguing-in-Publication Data

A CIP record for this book is available from the British Library.

Library of Congress Cataloging-in-Publication Data

Tyreman, C. J.
  How to master the IELTS : over 400 practice questions for all parts of the International English Language Testing System / Chris John Tyreman.
      p. cm.
   ISBN 978-0-7494-5636-8 – ISBN 978-0-7494-5946-8   1. International English Language Testing System. 2. English language–Textbooks for foreign speakers.   3. English language–Examinations–Study guides. I. Title.
   PE1128.T97 2012
   428.0076–dc23
                                                                          2011048826

Typeset by Graphicraft Ltd, Hong Kong
Printed and bound in India by Replika Press Pvt Ltd

Contents

General Reading and Writing Test A 103

General Reading and Writing Test B 117

Audio-Scripts for the Listening Tests 131

MP3 files for these tests can be downloaded for free at
www.koganpage.com/editions/how-to-master-the-ielts/9780749456368

Introduction

The IELTS is the world's most popular test with over 1.5 million people taking the test each year. It is intended for people who wish to study or work in an English-speaking country. You have the choice of two modules. The Academic module is for university degree course applicants. The General Training module is for people intending to migrate. This book contains four complete practice tests for the Academic module of the International English Testing Language System (IELTS) with additional tests for the General Training module. The tests provide IELTS candidates with plenty of realistic practice because they are similar in style and content to the University of Cambridge ESOL examinations.

Frequently Asked Questions (FAQs)

1. Where can I sit the IELTS?
You can sit the test in more than 130 countries at 800 test centres. Please visit the IELTS website at www.ielts.org to find a test centre near to you.

2. When can I sit the IELTS?
Tests are available every month of the year on fixed dates. There are 48 test dates for the Academic module and 24 test dates for the General module, but this does not mean that every centre offers a test on every date. The listening, reading and writing

tests are taken on the same day. The speaking test may be on the same day as the other three tests or it can be up to seven days before or seven days after.

3. How do I register for the IELTS?

To register for the test you need to download a copy of the IELTS application form (PDF file) or ask your test centre for a copy. You need to return:

- a completed and signed application form;

- your fee for the test (payment by credit/debit card is widely accepted; some centres accept online payments and some accept a cheque/postal order);

- a photocopy of your passport (or a photocopy of an EU National ID card);

- two identical, colour, passport-size photos that are less than six months old, and without glasses being worn.

4. How much does it cost to sit the IELTS?

The fee for the IELTS varies from one country to another. As a guide, the fee for the tests (both Academic and General) was £115 in the UK in 2011. Some countries accept online applications and payments.

5. What do I need to take to the exam?

You must take the following:

- a *valid* passport (or an EU National ID card), *not a photocopy*;

- at least two pens, two pencils, an eraser and a pencil sharpener (but no pencil case);

- water to drink, in a transparent bottle.

If you sit the speaking test separately – for example, the following week – you must take your ID again. You must not take your mobile phone into the examination room.

6. When are my results available?

Normally online 13 days after your test date. The official Test Report Form will also be mailed to your address after this time.

7. How many times can I sit the test?

You can sit the test again as many times as you like and as soon as you like, but you have to sit all four sections of the test. You cannot retake just one module again, for example the speaking test.

8. How long is the result valid for?

Your IELTS score is valid for two years. You may have to sit the test again if your test result is more than two years old.

9. What band score do I need?

The IELTS is scored from 0 to 9. You need to check with your university or institution what band score they need. University degree course applicants should aim for a band score of 7.0 or higher. The band score for people who wish to work and live in another country is usually 5.0 or higher.

10. What is the test format?

The test is split into four sections that cover the four key English skills of listening, reading, writing and speaking. The breakdown of the questions within each of the four sections is as follows:

- Listening Section (Academic *and* General modules) 40 questions

    - Four listening sections: 1, 2, 3 and 4, with 10 questions per section

    - Time allowed: 30 minutes.

- Reading Section (Academic module) 40 questions

    - Three reading passages: 1, 2 and 3, with 40 questions in total (eg 13, 13, 14)

    - Time allowed: 60 minutes.

- Writing Section (Academic module) 2 tasks

    - Task 1 (at least 150 words); eg describe the information in a graph or chart

    - Task 2 (at least 250 words); eg argumentative topic; reasons for and against

    - Time allowed: 60 minutes (eg 20 minutes on Task 1 and 40 minutes on Task 2).

- Reading Section (General Training module) 40 questions

  - Section 1: Two short texts of factual information; eg English in a social setting

  - Section 2: Two short texts of factual information; eg English in a work context

  - Section 3: One longer passage of text of general interest

  - Time allowed: 60 minutes.

- Writing Section (General Training module) 2 tasks

  - Task 1 (at least 150 words); eg write a letter on the chosen topic

  - Task 2 (at least 250 words); eg argumentative topic; reasons for and against

  - Time allowed: 60 minutes (eg 20 minutes on Task 1 and 40 minutes on Task 2).

- Speaking Section (Academic *and* General modules) 3 parts

  - Part 1: Familiar topics; Part 2: Brief talk; Part 3: Discussion

  - Time allowed: 11 to 14 minutes.

Book format

The questions in this book are numbered from 1 to 400 to make every answer easy to find. The main Answer section is found at the end of the book before the Appendices. There are two appendices: Appendix 1 is the Reading section vocabulary; Appendix 2 lists British and American spellings. The IELTS practice tests in this book are set out as follows:

Test 1: Questions 1 to 80; Test 2: Questions 81 to 160; Test 3: Questions 161 to 240; Test 4: Questions 241 to 320

General Training Reading and Writing Test A: Questions 321 to 360

General Training Reading and Writing Test B: Questions 361 to 400

Listening Test instructions

MP3 files for these tests can be downloaded for free at www.koganpage.com/editions/how-to-master-the-ielts/9780749456368

The IELTS practice tests in this book start with the Listening Test as does the actual test. Your CD player or computer must be able to play MP3 files. There are 16 separate recordings – four for each practice test. Section 1 is conversation between two people. Section 2 is a talk given by one person (monologue). Section 3 is a conversation between two or more people and Section 4 is another monologue. If you want to know more about what to expect then turn to the audio-scripts at the end of the book. Note that the answers to the listening tests have been underlined in the audio-scripts.

You will be allowed approximately 30 seconds to study the questions before the test begins. Use this time to check what types of answers are needed (for example, dates, times, names, money, etc), and pay special attention to the first question. Several sentences of dialogue may take place before you hear the words needed to answer the first question. If you miss the start point and fail to answer the first question you will not be ready to answer the second question. You will hear the recording only once, so if you think you have missed an answer you must move on to the next question. If you look at the audio-scripts you will see that each script is split into two parts separated by a dashed line; there is a 30-second gap at this point (first three scripts). Use these 30 seconds to read the next 10 questions. You will be given a piece of paper on which to write your answers. At the end of the listening module you will have 10 minutes to transfer your answers to the answer sheet. Finally, be aware that the Listening Test tests three skills of English language. You need to *listen* to the dialogue, *read* the questions and *write* the answers. Marks are needlessly lost when the candidate fails to read the instructions, or transfers them incorrectly to the answer sheet.

Example: write NO MORE THAN ONE WORD OR ONE NUMBER for each answer.

Question: How many weeks must be spent in the Halls of Residence?

Answer: 40 weeks x   Answer: 40 ✓

Example: write NO MORE THAN ONE WORD AND/OR A NUMBER for each answer.

> Question: How many weeks must be spent in the Halls of Residence?
>
> Answer: more than 40 x   Answer: 40 weeks ✓   Answer: 40 ✓

Target: aim for at least 30 correct answers out of 40 questions in these practice tests.

Reading Test instructions

You have one hour to complete 40 questions on three passages of text, or 20 minutes per test. Do not waste time reading the passage from beginning to end before looking at the questions. The reading test is a test of <u>word recognition</u> rather than a test of understanding. To answer many of the questions you need to look for a word or a string of words that have a similar meaning to those of the question. The word/words for your answer will <u>match with/map to</u> statements made in the passage. This means that you need to <u>study the first question carefully, then read the passage</u> of text, starting at the beginning. You can expect to arrive at the answer within a few sentences. The answer to the second question will come later in the passage and the answer to the third question will usually come later still, and so on. Example:

> Statement: <u>Changes</u> in the <u>earth's magnetic compass</u> can lead to <u>mistakes</u> in ...

Passage: The stranding of whales in shallow water and on beaches is not well understood but it can occur for entirely natural reasons. One explanation involves the ability of whales, like many animals, to use the earth's magnetic field for direction finding. Ocean currents are thought to cause <u>fluctuations</u> in the <u>earth's magnetic field</u> which may leave whales vulnerable to navigation <u>errors</u> when they migrate to their breeding ground.

Method: the word <u>mistakes</u> in the statement means the same as the word <u>errors</u> in the passage, so the answer is probably navigation; <u>mistakes in navigation</u> matches with <u>navigation errors</u>. Now check the rest of the sentence to confirm the match:

changes are the same as fluctuations and the earth's magnetic compass is the same as the earth's magnetic field, so the answer must be correct. Answer: navigation. An alternative word for navigation is 'direction', that is to say mistakes in direction, but this is wrong because the word 'direction' does not appear in the passage of text.

Target: aim for at least 30 correct answers out of 40 questions in these practice tests.

Writing Test instructions

If the question involves a graph or a chart (Task 1) make sure that you understand what the two axes show. Do not panic and become confused. Start by writing about one element of the chart (eg one line or one bar), choosing the largest first or the one with the largest change. Now move on to describe another element and make a comparison with the first element where there is an obvious difference. Continue like this with the remaining pieces of information. The timeline is always the bottom axis (x-axis) and the size is always the vertical axis (y-axis). The time reads from left to right and the size increases from bottom to top. To prepare for a question about a pie chart, make sure that you can describe the size of the portions in terms of simple fractions and percentages, for example: a half (50%), a third (33%), a quarter (25%), two thirds (67%), three quarters (75%). You can also make statements like 'just less than a half', or 'slightly more than a quarter', etc. If you have to describe a process, for example 'the natural water cycle', make sure that you identify the best point in the diagram to start your description; for example: Water leaves the surface of the earth by a process of evaporation. Now work logically to the next point in the process.

When writing about a topic (Task 2), read the question carefully. If the question asks you to 'discuss both views' then you need a balanced argument, so make a list of ideas for and against the issue, and then give your opinion (I believe; I think). Note that Task 2 counts for twice the marks of Task 1 so spend twice the amount of time on it. It is important to write at least 150 words for Task 1 and 250 words for Task 2. Make sure that you know roughly how much space this takes up with your hand-writing, otherwise you will waste time having to count your words.

Speaking Test instructions

You can practise for Part 1 by recording some information about yourself on a dictaphone, stating your name, where you live, what work you do and what hobbies and interests you have. You can also talk about your family and friends. Part 1 lasts between four and five minutes. For Part 2 you will be given a task card containing a general topic of interest and what you need to cover. You can make your own task cards from the Speaking Test questions in this book. Practise by recording your voice on a dictaphone and playing it back to check that it lasts between one and two minutes. Listen for pauses and hesitation, and check your pronunciation, grammar and vocabulary. In Part 3, the examiner will engage you in a conversation lasting between four and five minutes. Remember that you are not being assessed on your knowledge of the topic, only on your speech.

Ten top tips for IELTS

Listening section

1 Use the reading time to familiarize yourself with the types of answers expected; for example, a number, letter, word or time.

2 Pay special attention to the first question, so that you know when to begin.

3 If the question asks for answers with one word only, be careful not to add any extra word or letter by mistake. Pay special attention when choosing between similar numbers or clock times.

4 Copy your answers to the answer sheet exactly as you have written them. Make sure that your answers are written alongside the correct question numbers.

Reading section

5 You have 1 hour to complete 3 passages, so try to keep to 20 minutes per text.

6 Read the first question and then search for the sentence that contains the answer; it is often near the beginning of the passage.

Writing section

7 Write at least 150 words for Section 1 and at least 250 words for Section 2.

8 Spend about 20 minutes on Section 1 and 40 minutes on Section 2.

Speaking section

9 Practise speaking for 1 to 2 minutes on topics that are familiar to you.

10 Keep practising until you sound fluent.

TEST 1

Listening (1)

Section 1

Questions 1 to 5

Complete the notes below.

Write **NO MORE THAN ONE WORD AND/OR A NUMBER** for each answer.

Student accommodation

Options:

- Halls of Residence
  - £60 per week
  - self-catering
  - minimum stay **1** ....

- Student flats
  - owned by private landlords
  - at least £75 per week
  - need a reference and a **2** ....

- Homestay
  - owned by private landlords
  - minimum stay **3** ....
  - includes **4** .... and **5** ....

  Monday to Friday.

Questions 6 to 10

Complete the form below.

Write **NO MORE THAN TWO WORDS AND/OR A NUMBER** for each answer.

Homestay provision

Name: Mike **6** ....

Address: 108 Archer Park, Middleton, Manchester

Postcode: **7** ....

Tel. number: **8** ....

Smoker: No   **Cats:** Yes   **Dogs:** No

Special diet: Yes
(If Yes, please specify **9** ....)

Number of suitable providers identified: 10 ....

Details forwarded: Yes

Section 2

Questions 11 to 20

Look at the diagram and complete the list below it.

Write **NO MORE THAN THREE WORDS AND/OR A NUMBER** for each answer.

Campus plan for the Open Day

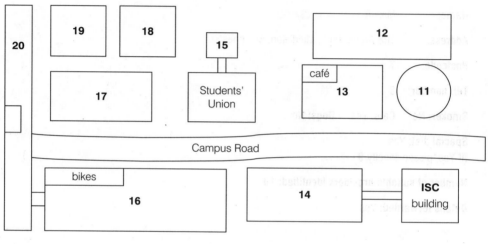

11	.... Centre ....
12	.... Hall ....
13	.... Room ....
14	.... Services ....
15	....
16	....
17	....
18	.... Hall ....
19	.... Hall ....
20	.... Road ....

Section 3

Questions 21 to 25

Choose the correct letter, **A**, **B** or **C**.

Numeracy week

21   According to the professor, the purpose of numeracy week is

    A   to draw attention to the advantages of better numeracy.

    B   to encourage young people to study more mathematics.

    C   to stress the importance of numerical skills.

22   According to the professor, there is a link between

    A   entering higher education and a better paid job.

    B   retraining and getting ahead in life.

    C   help with homework and doing well in school.

23   According to the professor, many people

    A   lack ability with words and numbers.

    B   are better at mathematics than they believe they are.

    C   have a very basic level of numeracy.

24   According to the professor, modern numeracy classes

    A   are mostly about basic arithmetic skills.

    B   cover maths for the workplace.

    C   concentrate on money matters.

25   The interviewer wonders if people return to education

    A   to prove themselves academically.

    B   to build confidence and self-esteem.

    C   to make up for failing at school.

Questions 26 to 30

Which skills does the professor say are important for learners?

Choose **THREE** letters from the list **A to G**.

A   calculator skills

B   times tables

C   equations

D   mental calculations

E   decimal numbers

F   algebra

G   measuring.

Questions 29 to 30

Complete the sentences below.

Write **ONE WORD ONLY** for each answer.

29   Some people find it difficult to read gauges on ....

30   Many employers use numeracy tests to eliminate the worst ....

Section 4

Complete the notes below..

Questions 31 to 40

Write **ONE WORD OR ONE NUMBER ONLY** for each answer.

Tropical storms

Different names

Some names are used in place of each other, which can create **31** ....

Tornado formation

Tornadoes form within thick **32** .... when warm air meets cold air.

Tornadoes become less frequent towards the **33** .... coast of America.

Cyclone formation

Cyclones form over oceans warmer than **34** .... degrees centigrade.

Cyclones rotate in the same direction as the **35** ....

Hurricanes and typhoons

A hurricane in America is called a typhoon in **36** ....

Questions 37 to 40

Write **NO MORE THAN THREE WORDS OR A NUMBER** for each answer.

Naming hurricanes

A hurricane is a tropical storm with a wind speed above **37** .... km/h

Before 1940, hurricanes were referred to by their **38** ....

After 1979, **39** .... names were chosen in turn.

Names can be reused after **40** .... years.

Reading (1)

Reading Passage 1

Shedding light on it

There are three main types of light bulb for lighting a room: incandescent, fluorescent and, more recently, the light emitting diode (LED) bulb. All three bulbs have their advantages and disadvantages when it comes to purchase price, running costs and environmental impact.

The traditional incandescent bulb has been in use for more than 100 years. It is made by suspending a fine coil of tungsten wire between two electrodes. When a current flows through the wire it reaches a temperature of more than 2,000°C and glows white hot. The bulb is filled with argon, an inert gas, to prevent the wire from evaporating. Traditional light bulbs are not very efficient, converting less than 10% of the energy into light with the rest as heat, making them too hot to handle. Most household light bulbs are rated at 40, 60 or 100 Watts.

Mass production of fluorescent lights began in the 1940s. The standard size is 1.2 m in length and 2.5 cm in diameter. The tube contains a small amount of mercury and the inside surface of the glass has a phosphor coating. There are two electrodes, one at each end of the tube, but there is no wire in between. Instead, mercury atoms absorb the electrical energy and emit ultraviolet (UV); this light is invisible until it hits the phosphor coating on the glass, which emits a visible white light. Fluorescent lights are about five times more efficient than incandescent light bulbs. A 20 Watt fluorescent tube will produce a similar amount of light to a 100 Watt bulb and runs much cooler, which helps to give it 10 times the life expectancy of a bulb.

The bright light produced by standard fluorescent lights makes them an ideal choice for offices and factories, rather than homes, where the incandescent bulb has traditionally reigned supreme. However, the newer compact fluorescent lamps (CFLs) look likely to make the old bulbs extinct. Global warming is the main reason. Compared with an incandescent bulb, a single energy-saving fluorescent lamp will save about one tonne of carbon-dioxide emissions over its lifetime, as well as reduce the consumer's electricity costs.

Not everybody likes the new CFLs, which have the following disadvantages: they are ten times the price of the traditional bulbs; flickering can occur with dimmer switches; they need to warm up to give full brightness; and they emit a bluish, less natural light that can strain the eye. Traditional bulbs are safer to dispose of because they are free from mercury, which is a neurotoxin. The mercury is safe inside a sealed CFL but it is released into the atmosphere if the bulb is broken. Mercury can accumulate in the body to attack the brain and central nervous system.

The reduced carbon footprint of CFLs in comparison with traditional bulbs may have been overstated. Whilst it is true that traditional bulbs convert 90% of the electricity into heat instead of light, this heat is not wasted. The bulb helps to keep the house warm so less fuel is burnt; for example, less gas or oil. If you change all your bulbs to CFLs it could prove very expensive in the short term and save less energy than you might imagine if your home is properly insulated or you live in a cold climate. If you live in a warm climate, then changing to CFLs will reduce your carbon footprint and the cost of your electricity bills, but the savings will be less than you might expect if the daylight hours are long and the nights are short.

CFLs are themselves under threat from the latest generation of light emitting diodes (LEDs). The LED has been in existence since the 1920s but they have only recently been made bright enough for room lighting. The most common applications to date have been traffic lights, solar garden lights and car brake lights; infrared LEDs are used in television remote controls. LEDs are electronic components that emit photons of light when the current is switched on. Lights for the home are made by clustering several LEDs into a single bulb.

Though more expensive than CFLs, LEDs last up to six times longer and are twice as efficient, producing the same amount of light from half the electrical power (half the carbon emissions). Other advantages of LED lighting include: an 'instant on', meaning that there is no warm-up time; no problems with frequent on/off switching, which shortens the life of fluorescent lights; no glass to break because the LED is made from a hard transparent plastic; and they are free from toxic mercury.

Questions 41 to 47

Do the following statements agree with the information given in Reading Passage 1? Write:

TRUE if the statement agrees with the information

FALSE if the statement contradicts the information

NOT GIVEN if there is no information on this.

41   Incandescent bulbs convert more energy to heat than light.

42   Ultraviolet light (UV) can be seen with the naked eye.

43   Compact fluorescent lamps (CFLs) last about 10 years.

44   Fluorescent tubes are the best lights for workplaces.

45   Incandescent bulbs contain mercury.

46   Fluorescent light can cause headaches and migraines.

47   Traditional bulbs may waste less energy than they appear to.

Questions 48 to 53

Complete the summary below.

Choose **NO MORE THAN TWO WORDS** from the passage for each answer.

Switching to CFLs may not be such a bright idea

Whilst it is true that compact fluorescent lamps (CFLs) have a smaller **48** .... than incandescent lighting, bulbs help to **49** .... the house, reducing the amount of gas or oil burnt. Consequently, the savings are less than expected in well **50** .... houses and in **51** .... regions. Fluorescent bulbs contain **52** ...., which is hazardous to health. The new light emitting diode (LED) bulbs carry no such risk and though expensive, they are more **53** .... than CFLs.

Reading Passage 2

Taking soundings

A Until recently it was thought that dolphins, porpoises and bats were the only mammals to use echolocation to locate prey and to navigate their environment. New research suggests that 'great whales', like the blue whale and the humpback whale, might be able to 'see' in a similar way. Underwater sound recordings of humpback whales have captured sonar clicks similar to those made by dolphins.

B The ability of 'great whales' to use sound to communicate has been known for decades. In deep water, where light cannot penetrate, whales use sound like we use our eyes. Low frequency vocalizations, in the form of grunts and moans are inaudible to the human ear, but form a pattern or song that enables whales to recognize their own species. Blue whales are the loudest animals on earth and their sounds can travel for hundreds of kilometres. Highly sensitive hearing allows whales to avoid shipping and to orientate themselves to the land by listening to waves crashing on the shore. Whales might also use sound to detect the seabed or polar ice packs by listening to the echoes of their own whale song. Man-made ocean sound, or 'noise pollution', can drown out whale calls. Increasing amounts of background noise from motorized shipping and from oil and gas drilling is making it difficult for whales to communicate and navigate via sound.

C Echolocation, also called bisonar, is a different form of sensory perception. A dolphin, for example, sends out a series of short clicks and waits for an echo to be reflected back from the obstacle or prey. Both the size and distance of an object can be determined from the echo. The clicks, known as ultrasound, consist of high-pitch (frequency) sound waves, well above the range of the human ear, and distinct from the low-pitched whale song. Whilst there is evidence supporting the use of ultrasound by whales, it has not been shown that they can use echolocation. Instead, the clicks might serve to scare and control shoals of small fish on which some whales prey.

D A major concern of environmentalists is that high-power military sonar might dis-orientate or harm whales, and that it is responsible for the mass strandings seen on beaches. However, whales were beaching themselves before the invention of sonar and evidence from fossils indicates that stranding goes back thousands of years. Today though, stranding occurs more frequently in waters where navy training exercises take place. The impact of man-made sonar on the stranding of whales and dolphins can no longer be ignored. Following pressure from environmentalists, US law requires that the navy take steps to minimize the effects of sonar on mammals wherever possible. Most of these precautions are common sense and include avoiding whale migration routes when whales are present, not operating the sonar when dolphins are riding a bow wave, and checking to see if a stranding has taken place after sonar has been deployed.

E The phenomenon of stranding is not well understood but it can occur for entirely natural reasons. One explanation involves the ability of whales, like many animals, to use the earth's magnetic field for direction finding. Ocean currents are thought to cause fluctuations in the earth's magnetic field, which may leave whales vulnerable to navigation errors when they migrate to their breeding grounds. Other reasons for stranding include straying into shallow coastal water when following prey, or when attempting to escape predators such as killer whales. Sea currents, winds and storms are all known to play their part. When a single whale is found dead on a beach it might have died from natural causes out at sea and been washed up on shore. It is apparent that multiple deaths at sea cannot produce a 'mass stranding' on a single beach because the carcases would have washed up along different parts of the shoreline. In these circumstances there is concern that the multiple deaths may be man-made, linked to marine pollution, over-fishing, which deprives the whales of food, or entanglement with nets. However, a mass stranding of whales on a single beach, like those shown on television, can also arise naturally. Whales are social animals that swim in groups known as 'pods'. Some scientists have speculated that if a sick or injured whale takes refuge in shallower water the rest of the pod might follow on to become trapped when the tide goes out.

Questions 54 to 58

Reading Passage 2 has five paragraphs **A to E**.

Which paragraph contains the following information?

Write **A**, **B**, **C**, **D** or **E**. You may use any letter more than once.

54   an example of sound being used other than for navigation and location of prey

55   examples of mammals other than whales and dolphins that use echolocation

56   how man's behaviour has increased the number of whales being stranded

57   an example of whales living in a community

58   why people cannot hear whale song.

Questions 59 to 62

Complete the summary below.

Choose **NO MORE THAN TWO WORDS** from the passage for each answer.

The harmful effects of high-power sonar on whales are a **59** .... It is recognized that the navy pose a threat to whales during **60** .... when the number of beachings have been observed to increase. The impact of sonar on mammals can be lessened by taking a number of **61** .... steps. For example, it is clear that ships with sonar equipment should keep away from whale **62** ....

Questions 63 to 66

Complete the summary below.

Choose **ONLY ONE WORD** from the passage for each answer.

Several reasons, not linked with human activities, have been proposed to explain why whales beach themselves. Changes in the earth's magnetic compass can lead to mistakes in **63** .... Alternatively, whales might stray into shallow water when pursued by **64** .... , or to chase prey, and then become trapped by the tide. Whilst one whale on a beach might have died naturally out at sea and been washed ashore, a group of whales **65** .... because their bodies would appear on different stretches of sand. 'Mass stranding' appears to be linked to the **66** .... nature of whales and their tendency to swim into shallow water as a group.

Reading Passage 3

Oxbridge

Although more than 100 km separates the English cities of Oxford and Cambridge, their universities are linked by the term 'Oxbridge'. It is a name that can be applied to either university or to both. Traditionally, a degree at Oxbridge symbolized the pinnacle of academic achievement. Cities like Birmingham, Liverpool, Bristol and Manchester had their own universities, but these were not as esteemed as Oxbridge and received the derogatory title of 'Red brick' universities. In recent times, the name Oxbridge has also become a derogatory term. Some people believe that Oxbridge is part of a social class system that favours the privileged few, born into wealth or high social status, at the expense of the less well-off, socially disadvantaged, though equally talented students. Whilst Oxford and Cambridge encourage applications from candidates living in deprived areas, only 1 in 100 of the poorest university students in England received an Oxbridge education in 2010, far lower than the percentage of poorer students at the 'Red brick' universities.

It cannot be disputed that a disproportionate number of Oxbridge entrants went to a fee-paying private school rather than to a free, state school. Nationally, only 1 in 15 pupils receive a private education, but nearly half of the students at Oxbridge went to a private school. Fee-paying schools have higher staff-to-pupil ratios, so their pupils receive more tuition and achieve higher grades than pupils from state sector schools. It is surely no surprise that pupils with an education paid for by their parents are about 20 times more likely to be offered a place at Oxbridge. There is no reason to believe that the best pupils in the state sector are any less intelligent than those in the private sector. Given the same educational opportunities and life circumstances, state sector pupils can achieve equally high grades. The failure of the best pupils to achieve their potential can often be linked to a difficult home life, lack of motivation or peer pressure from less academic pupils. The attainment gap between university applicants from fee-paying and state schools is maintained when Oxbridge graduates are rewarded with the best-paying jobs, affording them the opportunity to send their own children to the best schools.

Looked at from the perspective of life chances, Oxbridge helps to maintain the 'social divide' where the rich get richer and the poor remain poor. Some people would argue that this 'Oxbridge advantage' is a symptom of social stratification rather than a cause of it. After all, parents cannot be blamed for wanting the best education for their children and Oxbridge cannot be held responsible for the failure of state schools to achieve the necessary grades. There is no evidence to suggest that

Oxbridge selects students on anything other than merit. Indeed, in some subjects the application process includes admissions and aptitude tests that help to ensure a level playing field. Perhaps then, the state sector needs to encourage and support more applications from their best pupils to the best universities. Alternatively, the low aspiration of some pupils' parents may fail to drive gifted pupils onwards and upwards, or it may be that some pupils from an ordinary background are not comfortable with the idea of attending Oxbridge. Students who do not feel that they will 'fit in' at Oxbridge can still make the most of their talents by attending one of the country's many other excellent universities.

Inequalities in our society do not begin and end with Oxbridge. The best state schools are usually found in the most affluent areas. Injustices can arise when parents move house to secure a child's place at a more desirable school and in doing so they force another child into an under-performing school. Other, better-off parents, though not necessarily wealthy, will pay for their children to be educated at a private school to avoid having to move home. Either way, the desire to furnish one's children with the best possible education outweighs any sense of social justice. Unless remedies can be found for the disparity in educational standards in the pre-university years, it is unrealistic to believe that Oxbridge contributes in any substantial way to a lack of social mobility. A place at Oxbridge should be seen as an opportunity for self-improvement and learning at the highest standards whatever one's social background.

Questions 67 to 70

Choose the correct letter **A**, **B**, **C** or **D** for the questions based on Reading Passage 3.

67 In the past Oxbridge has been seen as

    A an education only for those who can afford to pay for it.

    B the best universities in the country.

    C an opportunity for learning and self-improvement.

    D a place that represents the highest educational standards.

68 Everybody agrees that

    A too many Oxbridge students have had a private education.

    B there are higher staff to student ratios at Oxbridge.

    C life at Oxbridge is for those with money and social status.

    D Oxbridge applicants are rewarded with the best degrees.

69   In the passage, there is an example of how Oxbridge

    A   encourages applications from pupils living in deprived areas.

    B   has made the application process fairer.

    C   selects students based on their exam results.

    D   maintains its advantage over other universities.

70   In the passage, a link is made between a degree at Oxbridge and

    A   inequalities in state schools.

    B   a pupil's aspiration.

    C   a successful career.

    D   under-performing schools.

Questions 71 to 76

Do the following statements agree with the information given in Reading Passage 3? Write:

TRUE if the statement agrees with the information

FALSE if the statement contradicts the information

NOT GIVEN if there is no information on this.

71   The 'Oxbridge advantage' refers to better prospects in life.

72   Some Oxbridge candidates are offered a place whether they deserve it or not.

73   A student from an ordinary background is unlikely to do well at Oxbridge.

74   A lack of applications from state schools is the only reason for the low number of state school students at Oxbridge.

75   The author does not believe that Oxbridge is responsible for social inequalities.

76   There are few good schools in the state sector.

Questions 77 to 80

Complete the following summary using the list of words, **A to K**, below.

The best schools tend to be found in the most **77** .... areas. This leads to a lack of **78** .... in the state school system. For example, some parents will move closer to a better-performing state school, or failing this, pay for their children to be educated **79** .... Children from poorer families can lose out, but the desire for one's children to do well at school is more **80** .... than any sense of social justice.

A deprived	**B** valuable	**C** quality	**D** fairness	**E** applicants	**F** advantaged
G important	**H** privately	**I** prosperous	**J** selectively	**K** preferentially	

Writing (1)

Writing task 1

You should spend about 20 minutes on this task.

The graph shows the percentage of four different types of fuels in use between the years 1800 and 2000.

Summarize the information by describing the main features of the graph and making comparisons where appropriate.

Write at least 150 words.

Fuel usage 1800 to 2000

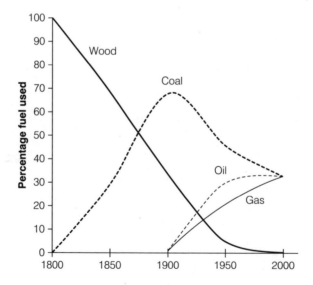

Writing task 2

You should spend about 40 minutes on this task.

Write about the following topic.

> **Some people believe that electronic calculators should not be allowed in school until after the pupils have mastered mental arithmetic. Others believe that calculators save pupils time, especially with complicated calculations.**
>
> **Discuss both these views and give your own opinion.**

Give reasons for your answer and include any relevant examples from your own knowledge or experience.

Write at least 250 words.

Speaking (1)

Part 1 Familiar topics

Hobbies

- What do you do with your free time? [Why?]
  I like to .... (present tense) because

- Which activity do you enjoy most? [Why?]
  Mostly I enjoy (present tense) ....

- How much time do you spend on it? [When?]
  Usually I spend (present tense) ....

- What hobbies can your family do? [Who?]
  My mother can (present tense) ....

Part 2 Brief talk

I want you to talk about a topic I'm going to give you. You have one minute to think about what you are going to say. You can make some notes to help you. Your talk should last between one and two minutes.

Talk about the type of food you like

[What is your favourite food?] .... [What don't you like?] .... [Is it traditional for your country?] .... [What are the ingredients?] .... [Are they healthy?] ....
[Who cooks your food?]

How do your meals compare with restaurant food?

Part 3 Discussion

Convenience food

Do you think that people eat too much fast food and takeaways?

Do you eat fast food? [Why? When? How often?] Yes, I'm fond of . . . .

Do you like microwave meals? [Why?] Sometimes, when I'm in a hurry . . . .

What are the problems with eating fast food? [Why?] It can be unhealthy because . . . .

Would you say that you eat healthily? [Why?] Yes I would, but . . . .

Tip: If you make a mistake with your grammar (eg you use a present tense verb instead of past tense verb) and you know how to correct it then do so.

TEST 2

Listening (2)

Section 1

Questions 81 to 85

Complete the notes below.

Write **NO MORE THAN TWO WORDS AND/OR A NUMBER** for each answer.

Walking tour

Booked on: **81** .... Tour

Booked for:
- 14.00 hrs
- Friday
- **82** ....

Debit card number: xxxx xxxx xxxx xxxx

Full name: Dave **83** ....

Spaces reserved for **84** .... people

Amount paid: **85** ....

Questions 86 to 90

Complete the form below.

Write **NO MORE THAN TWO WORDS AND/OR A NUMBER** for each answer.

Revised booking

Booked on: Inspector Morse Tour

Booked for:

- 13.45 hrs
- Saturday
- **86** ....

Additional charge: **87** ....

Debit card number: **88** ....

Booking reference number: **89** ....

Name of guide: **90** ....

Section 2

Questions 91 to 96

Choose the correct letter, **A**, **B** or **C**.

Field trip

91   What proportion of students achieved a high mark in their assignments?

A

B

C

92   Accommodation is required for

    A 6 nights

    B 7 nights

    C 8 nights

93   The ferry arrives at

    A 02.40 hrs

    B 06.00 hrs

    C 07.30 hrs

94   Halfway to the ferry there will be a short stop

    A for food and drink

    B to use the toilets

    C both A and B

95   On leaving the vehicle deck, students should take

    A few personal items

    B all personal items

    C important personal items

96   The village of Dundrum has a

    A Roman fort

    B Norman castle

    C Tower house

Questions 97 to 100

Complete the notes below.

Write **ONE WORD ONLY** for each answer.

TABLE 2.1

FIELD TRIP TIMETABLE	
Day 1	lunch followed by a walk by the **97** ....
Day 2	spend all day in the mountains visit a reservoir visit the town then go for a walk in a **98** ....
Day 3	travel to Portrush visit the Giants Causeway cross a bridge made from **99** ....
Day 4	day of rest visit to a brewery in the afternoon
Day 5	travel to Londonderry visit Glenelly valley
Day 6	travel to Ballycastle see **100** .... on the cliffs

Section 3

Questions 101 to 105

Complete the flow chart below.

Write **ONE WORD/NUMBER ONLY** for each answer.

Poster presentation

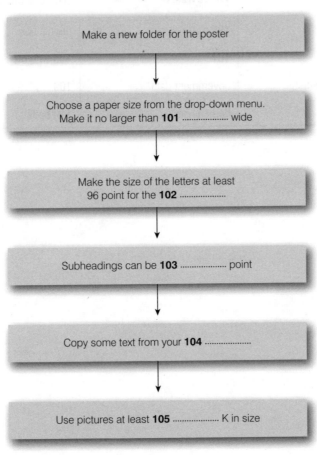

Make a new folder for the poster

↓

Choose a paper size from the drop-down menu.
Make it no larger than **101** .... wide

↓

Make the size of the letters at least
96 point for the **102** ....

↓

Subheadings can be **103** .... point

↓

Copy some text from your **104** ....

↓

Use pictures at least **105** .... K in size

Questions 106 to 110

Complete the table below.

Write **NO MORE THAN TWO WORDS** for each answer.

TABLE 2.2

Information/picture	Where from?	Where in the poster?
carbon offsetting	**106** a	middle box
carbon cycle	**107**	**108** with the . . . .
carbon emissions	government data	**109** . . . . box
college logo	home page	**110** both . . . .

Section 4

Questions 111 to 116

Choose the correct letter, **A**, **B** or **C**.

History of diagrams

111 According to the professor, ancient pictures of wild animals are

A found in Europe only.
B found in Australia only.
C found in both Europe and Australia.

112 According to the professor, Egyptian hieroglyphics are

A difficult to understand.
B language in pictures.
C decorative drawings.

113 According to the professor, Pythagoras and Archimedes were both

A mathematicians.
B scientists.
C astronomers.

114 According to Wikipedia, a map is a diagram

A with axes and co-ordinates.
B of part of the earth's surface.
C that links one place to another.

115 According to the professor, modern diagrams

A are charts or graphs only.
B contain more information than text.
C help to explain complicated data.

116 According to the professor, Florence Nightingale used a chart

A similar to a pie chart.
B identical to a pie chart.
C different to a pie chart.

Questions 117 to 120

Complete the notes below.

Write **NO MORE THAN ONE WORD** for each answer.

Flow charts

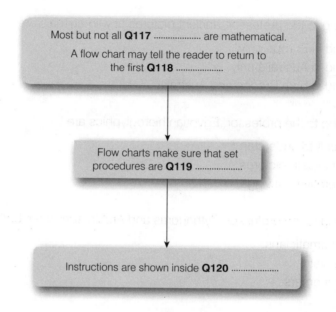

Most but not all **Q117** .... are mathematical.

A flow chart may tell the reader to return to the first **Q118** ....

Flow charts make sure that set procedures are **Q119** ....

Instructions are shown inside **Q120** ....

Reading (2)

Reading Passage 4

Rosetta Stone

In 1799, a famous discovery was made in the small town of Rashid (known as Rosette by the French), 65 km from the city of Alexandria in northern Egypt. Napoleon Bonaparte's army were digging the foundations of a fort when they unearthed a large basalt slab, over 1.1 metres tall, 75 cm wide and 28 cm thick, weighing about 760 kg.

The 'Pierre de Rosette' (Rosetta Stone) dates back to 196 BC when the Macedonians ruled Egypt. The stone is of great historical value because it is carved with the same text written in two Ancient Egyptian scripts (hieroglyphics and Demotic) and in Greek. At the time of the discovery, Egyptian hieroglyphic writing could not be understood, and by comparing the symbols with the Greek text it was eventually deciphered. This allowed scholars to understand the meaning of Egyptian hieroglyphs dating back almost 4,000 years.

Napoleon was defeated by the British navy in the battle of the Nile in 1798 and he left Egypt two years later. The Rosetta Stone, together with other antiquities, was handed over to the British under the terms of the Treaty of Alexandria in 1801. It went on display in the British Museum and to this day remains one of the most popular exhibits. In 1802, Thomas Young, an English academic, translated some of the words in the Demotic section of the stone. Despite this early success, he made little headway with the hieroglyphic symbols, which proved baffling. The problem remained largely unsolved for a further 20 years until the French scholar, Jean-Francois Champollian, unlocked the code. He realized that the symbols used a combination of alphabet letters and phonetic sounds to convey the same meaning as the classical Greek writing. In 1828 he travelled to Egypt where he was able to read hieroglyphs off temple walls, obelisks and other ancient artefacts to establish, for the first time, the order of kings, when they ruled and how they lived. Champollian is acknowledged as the father of modern Egyptology.

The Rosetta Stone has revealed its secrets. The hieroglyphs were written on the stone by Egyptian priests to proclaim the greatness of their Pharaohs, in this case, 13-year-old King Ptolemy V, the fifth ruler of the Ptolemaic dynasty, and son of Ptolemy IV. The stone was made on the first anniversary of the boy king's coronation in 197 BC and takes the form of a decree. It affirms the rightful place of Ptolemy V as the King of Egypt and instructs the priests to worship him and erect temples. The Demotic language was used in daily life in Egypt, and the classical Greek by the ruling Ptolemies, so it made sense to have these languages on the stone as well as the hieroglyphs so that the decree could be understood by everyone. The stone is not unique in that similar stones would have been placed at other Egyptian temples.

In recent times, Egypt's head of antiquities, Dr Zahi Hawass, has lobbied for the return of the Rosetta Stone to Egypt, along with other prized antiquities like the 'Elgin Marbles' and the bust of Queen Nefertiti. The repatriation of artefacts of cultural heritage is a controversial and emotive issue. The problem is in deciding between what was taken on a fair basis and what was stolen. However, in 2002, 30 of the world's leading museums issued the joint declaration that 'objects acquired in earlier times must be viewed in the light of different sensitivities and values reflective of that earlier era'. Whilst this statement may suit the many museums that wish to conserve historically important artefacts, some of the objects are held sacred by the peoples and nations from which they originate. In the case of the Rosetta Stone, the British Museum donated a life-size replica of the stone to the town of Rashid (Rosetta) in 2005 and a giant copy in France marks the birthplace of Jean-Francois Champollian. Though not authentic items, these copies provide an opportunity for study and learning. The British Museum will loan treasured artefacts to other museums around the world, though in doing so it runs the risk of not getting them back.

Today the term 'Rosetta Stone' has been adopted by a language-learning company and is more likely to be recognized in this context than as an important cultural artefact. The term is also used as a metaphor for anything that is vital to unlocking a difficult problem, for example, DNA has become the 'Rosetta Stone of life and death, health and disease', according to the Human Genome Project. Nevertheless, it is the science of Egyptology that carries on the legacy of the Rosetta Stone.

Questions 121 to 128

Do the following statements agree with the information given in Reading Passage 4?

Write:

TRUE if the statement agrees with the information

FALSE if the statement contradicts the information

NOT GIVEN if there is no information on this.

121 The Rosetta Stone was unearthed in the city of Alexandria.

122 There are three translations of the same passage on the Rosetta Stone.

123 Egyptian scholars wrote the passages almost 4,000 years ago.

124 Thomas Young translated the entire Demotic text.

125 The hieroglyphs were more difficult to translate than the Demotic text.

126 Demotic language used phonetic sounds.

127 Jean-Francois Champollian is the founder of the science of Egyptology.

128 The Rosetta Stone was the only stone of its type.

Questions 129 to 133

Complete each sentence with the correct ending, **A** to **J**, below.

129 The head of Egypt's antiquities believes

130 The return of antiquities to their country of origin is a topic

131 In 2002, 30 museums stated

132 Where prized artefacts are concerned, there is a danger

133 Rosetta Stone is a name

A   that all items of cultural heritage should be repatriated.
B   that the taking of antiquities cannot be judged by today's standards.
C   that is associated more with language training than with antiquities.
D   that was used by the French army.
E   that the country's treasured antiquities belong in Egypt.
F   that reflects the values of an earlier period.
G   that provokes debate and generates strong feelings.
H   that some of the objects are held sacred.
I   that borrowed items will not be conserved and protected.
J   that borrowed items will be kept and not returned.

Reading Passage 5

Tickled pink

In 1973, the Australian fruit breeder John Cripps created a new variety of apple tree by crossing a red Australian Lady Williams variety with a pale-green American Golden Delicious. The offspring first fruited in 1979 and combined the best features of its parents in an apple that had an attractive pink hue on a yellow undertone. The new, improved apple was named the Cripps Pink after its inventor.

Today the Cripps Pink is one of the most popular varieties of apple and is grown extensively in Australia, New Zealand, Canada, France and in California and Washington in the USA. By switching from northern hemisphere fruit to southern hemisphere fruit the apple is available at its seasonal best all year round. The highest-quality apples are marketed worldwide under the trademark Pink Lady™. To preserve the premium price and appeal of the Pink Lady, apples that fail to meet the highest standards are sold under the name Cripps Pink™. These standards are based on colour and flavour, in particular, the extent of the pink coverage and the sugar/acid balance. Consumers who buy a Pink Lady apple are ensured a product that is of consistently high quality.

To earn the name Pink Lady the skin of a Cripps Pink apple must be at least 40% pink. Strong sunlight increases the pink coloration and it may be necessary to remove the uppermost leaves of a tree to let the light through. The extra work required to cultivate Cripps Pink trees is offset by its advantages, which include: vigorous trees; fruit that has tolerance to sunburn; a thin skin that does not crack; flesh that is resistant to browning after being cut and exposed to air; a cold-storage life of up to six months and a retail shelf-life of about four weeks. However, the main advantage for apple growers is the premium price that the Pink Lady brand is able to command.

The Cripps Red variety, also known as Cripps II, is related to the Pink Lady and was developed at the same time. The premium grade is marketed as the Sundowner™. Unlike the genuinely pink Pink Lady, the Sundowner™ is a classic bi-coloured apple, with a skin that is 45% red from Lady Williams and 55% green from Golden Delicious. Apples that fall outside of this colour ratio are rejected at the packing station and used for juice, whilst the smaller apples are retained for the home market. The Sundowner is harvested after Cripps Pink in late May or early June, and a few weeks before Lady Williams. It has better cold-storage properties than Cripps Pink and it retains an excellent shelf life. Cripps Red apples have a coarser texture than Cripps Pink, are less sweet and have a stronger flavour. Both apples are sweeter than Lady Williams but neither is as sweet as Golden Delicious.

The advantage of the Pink Lady™ brand is that it is a trademark of a premium product, not just a Cripps Pink apple. This means that new and improved strains of the Cripps Pink can use the Pink Lady brand name as long as they meet the minimum quality requirement of being 40% pink. Three such strains are the Rosy Glow, The Ruby Pink and the Lady in Red. The Rosy Glow apple was discovered in an orchard of Cripps Pink trees that had been planted in South Australia in 1996. One limb of a Cripps Pink tree had red-coloured apples while the rest of the limbs bore mostly green fruit. A bud was taken from the mutated branch and grafted onto rootstock to produce the new variety. The fruit from the new Rosy Glow tree was the same colour over the entire tree and a patent for this unique apple was granted in 2003. The Rosy Glow apple benefits from a larger area of pink than the Pink Lady and it ripens earlier in the season in climates that have less hours of sunshine. As a consequence, the Cripps Pink is likely to be phased out in favour of the Rosy Glow, with the apples branded as Pink Lady™ if they have 40% or more pink coverage.

Ruby Pink and Lady in Red are two mutations of the Cripps Pink that were discovered in New Zealand. Like the Rosy Glow, these improved varieties develop a larger area of pink than the Cripps Pink, which allows more apples to meet the quality requirements of the Pink Lady™ brand. Planting of these trees may need to be controlled otherwise the supply of Pink Lady apples will exceed the demand, to then threaten the price premium. Overproduction apart, the future of what has become possibly the world's best-known modern apple and fruit brand, looks secure.

Questions 134 to 139

Do the following statements agree with the information given in Reading Passage 5?

Write:

TRUE if the statement agrees with the information

FALSE if the statement contradicts the information

NOT GIVEN if there is no information on this.

134 Pink Lady apples are the highest grade of Cripps Pink apples.

135 One advantage of Cripps Pink trees is that they grow well.

136 Cripps Pink trees produce an abundance of fruit.

137 Pink Lady apples are less expensive to buy than Cripps Pink apples.

138 Colour is an important factor in the selection of both of the premium grades of Cripps apples referred to.

139 Lady Williams apples are sweeter than Golden Delicious.

Questions 140 to 144

Complete the summary below.

Choose **NO MORE THAN TWO WORDS** from the passage for each answer.

New and improved strains

A bud taken from a mutated branch on a Cripps Pink tree was grafted onto rootstock to produce the new apple variety named **140** .... A feature of this improved apple is that it **141** .... sooner than the Pink Lady with less sun. Another mutated strain is the **142** .... tree from New Zealand. The chief advantage of new and improved strains is that the apples develop more **143** .... so more can use the name **144** ....

Questions 145 to 147

Identify the following apples as being:

    A Pink Lady

    B Sundowner

    C Lady in Red

    D Lady Williams

145 The trademark of the highest-quality Cripps Red apple.

146 Not as sweet as either Cripps Red or Cripps Pink apples.

147 A mutation of a Cripps Pink tree.

Reading Passage 6

Bubbly and burgers

When is Champagne not Champagne? The answer is when it is sparkling wine produced outside the Champagne region of France. Unfair trading is a breach of civil law that covers unfair practices towards consumers. Customers are misled into believing that they are buying goods or services associated with a well-known, more established business, through the use of confusingly similar trademarks or trade names. In the UK, unfair trading is known as 'passing off' and in the USA as 'palming off'. The protection of a trading name is essential for an established business because associations with a lesser firm can damage a company's reputation. Nevertheless, some businesses still try to bolster trade by incorporating descriptive elements or imagery from better known, more attractive brands, into their own signs and logos.

The Champagne growers of France have successfully defended the Champagne brand against any sparkling wine produced outside the Champagne region. So, for example, you will not find any Spanish Champagne on the shelves, only Cava. Other sparkling wines barred from describing themselves as Champagne include: Asti (Italy); Espumante (Portugal); Sekt (Germany); and Shiraz (Australia). Sparkling French wines made outside of the Champagne region are termed Crenmant and Mousseaux. All these 'copycat' sparkling wines are made by the traditional Champagne method, in which case they are permitted to state Methode Traditionelle on the label. In the traditional method, the fizz is obtained via a secondary fermentation process inside a sealed bottle. In a budget sparkling wine, the fizz is generated artificially by injecting high-pressure carbon-dioxide gas into still wine prior to bottling, as per carbonated drinks. Carbonated wines release large bubbles to develop foam that rises and subsides quickly, whereas Champagne releases uniquely fine bubbles that rise slowly to create long-lasting foam.

The defence of the Champagne name has not been entirely successful. Elderflower 'Champagne' is a favourite non-alcoholic summer drink in the UK. It self-ferments to produce Champagne-like foam when the bottle is opened. In 1993, the Thorncroft Vineyards in Surrey, England, successfully defended a passing-off lawsuit when the judge deemed that the risk of damage to the reputation of genuine Champagne was negligible, even though Thorncroft had presented the drink in a champagne-style bottle with a wired cork. Despite this initial ruling, the decision was overturned in an appeal case a few months later. The judges felt that consumers might believe that the drink was a non-alcoholic version of Champagne, and that to maintain its exclusiveness, only authentic Champagne could describe itself as Champagne. Other drinks manufacturers have found it necessary to protect their brand's identities by invoking the passing-off law. Sherry and Port are names that are restricted to fortified wines that emanate from Jerez in Spain, and the Douro Valley in Portugal, respectively. Warninks Advocaat is a traditional egg and brandy liqueur made in Holland since 1616, which Keeling's Old English Advocaat failed to usurp in 1979. In 2010, Diageo Smirnoff Vodka prevented Intercontinental Brands from selling a cheaper vodka-containing drink named Vodkat, primarily because it did not contain the necessary 37.5% alcohol to be classed as vodka.

A passing-off claim is likely to succeed in circumstances where the consumer might be deceived into purchasing a product that is similar to that of a claimant who has a strong brand identity and a reputation to protect, that is to say, there is a risk of damage to the claimant's 'goodwill'. A passing-off claim is less likely to succeed when the defendant is innocently using his or her own name, or the claimant's product and labelling are not distinct enough to distinguish it as only belonging to them. Norman McDonald ran a small restaurant named McDonald's Hamburgers Country drive-in. He fell foul of the McDonald's restaurant chain by including two lit golden arches in his sign. He was forced to remove the arches and add Norman in front of McDonald's on the sign, so as not to misrepresent the business as a McDonald's franchise.

McDonald's has taken legal action against several businesses that refused to drop Mc from their trading name, including those with very similar names, such as MacDonald's and Mcdonald. McDonald's have not always won their legal cases. However, they were more likely to succeed if the defendants had a clear association with a food service that could be confused with McDonald's. So a fast-food outlet in the Philippines named MacJoy was forced to change its name and became MyJoy; Elizabeth McCaughey had to alter the name of her coffee shop from McCoffee, which was a play on her name; and a Scottish sandwich-shop owner was restrained from using the name McMunchies; but McChina Wok Away was permitted because it was ruled that McChina would not cause any confusion amongst customers. It was also indicated that McDonald's did not have exclusive rights to the prefix Mc. This was confirmed when McDonalds lost its case against McCurry despite an earlier ruling that the prefix Mc, combined with colours distinctive of the McDonald's brand, might confuse and deceive customers. The business had claimed that McCurry stood for Malaysian Chicken Curry.

Questions 148 to 151

Choose the correct letter **A**, **B**, **C** or **D** for the questions based on Reading Passage 6.

148 The passage 'Bubbly and burgers' is mainly concerned with

A   Champagne and McDonald's.
B   'copycat' food and drink.
C   the impact of 'passing off' on trade.
D   the meaning of 'passing off'.

149 In the passage, the author states that sparkling wine

A   is not Champagne unless it originates from the Champagne region.
B   is often passed off as authentic Champagne.
C   is not allowed to state Methode Traditionelle on the label.
D   is carbonated by injecting it with carbon-dioxide gas.

150 In the passage, the author states that Elderflower 'Champagne'

A   is a non-alcoholic Champagne.
B   is similar to Champagne in the foam it produces.
C   is a popular low-alcohol summer drink.
D   is a favourite carbonated fruit drink.

151 The passage indicates that Norman McDonald

A   falsely represented his business as a McDonald's franchise.
B   innocently used his own surname to increase trade.
C   was forced to remove the name McDonald's from the sign.
D   used two lit arches indistinguishable from the McDonald's logo.

Questions 152 to 155

Do the following statements agree with the information given in Reading Passage 6?

Write:

TRUE if the statement agrees with the information

FALSE if the statement contradicts the information

NOT GIVEN if there is no information on this.

152 Passing off and palming off are different breaches of civil law.

153 Champagne production involves two fermentation processes.

154 Inexpensive sparkling wines are carbonated naturally inside the bottle.

155 Elderflower 'Champagne' is a popular summer drink in several EU countries.

Questions 156 to 160

Complete the sentences below.

Choose **NO MORE THAN THREE WORDS** from the passage for each answer.

156 In 1993, Thorncroft won a lawsuit because it was deemed that Champagne's reputation was at .... of being damaged.

157 Vodkat was banned mainly because it contained insufficient ....

158 McDonald's, Macdonald and Mcdonald are ....

159 McDonald's were more likely to win their cases if the defendants had obvious links with .... similar to McDonald's.

160 A ruling indicated that the rights to use the prefix Mc were .... to McDonald's.

Writing (2)

Writing task 1

You should spend about 20 minutes on this task.

The pie charts below show the percentage of housing owned and rented in the UK in 1985 and 2005.

Summarize the information by describing the main features of the charts and making comparisons where appropriate.

Write at least 150 words.

Housing owned and rented in the UK

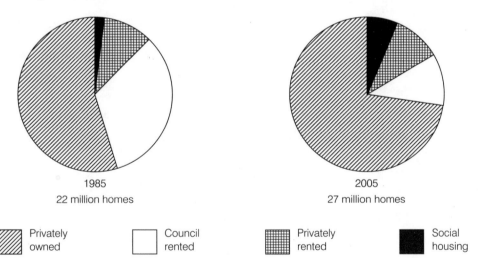

1985
22 million homes

2005
27 million homes

Privately owned

Council rented

Privately rented

Social housing

Writing Task 2

You should spend about 40 minutes on this task.

Some people believe that unemployed people should be made to work for their welfare/benefit payments. Others, however, see this as cheap labour.

Discuss the possible advantages and disadvantages of making unemployed people take any job.

Do you believe that making unemployed people work is a good idea?

Give reasons for your answer and include any relevant experience or knowledge.

Write at least 250 words.

Speaking (2)

Part 1 Familiar topics

Travelling to work

- How do you get to work/college?
  I usually travel (present tense) by ....

- Do you enjoy the journey? [Why?/Why not?]
  No I don't (present tense) because ....

- Have you ever been late for work/college? [Why?]
  Yes I have been. I was (past tense) last month when the train was delayed
  (past tense).

- What happened when you arrived? [Why?]
  My boss was (unhappy) because ....

Part 2 Brief talk

I want you to talk about a topic I'm going to give you. You have one minute to think
about what you are going to say. You can make some notes to help you. Your talk
should last between **one and two minutes**.

Talk about the place where you live.

[What is it called?] [Where is it?] [How big is it?]

[Who lives there?] [Are they friendly?]

[Shops] [Services] [Transport]

How does it compare with other places you have lived?

Part 3 Discussion

Choosing where to live

Some people prefer to live in a big city and others prefer to live in a small town.

Which do you prefer?

What are the benefits of living there? [Why?]

What are the disadvantages of living there? [Why?]

Do you think that the standard of living is higher in a big city? [Why?]

Tip: for a higher mark, try to speak at a normal speed without hesitating to find the right word or grammar.

TEST 3

Listening (3)

Section 1

Questions 161 to 170

Complete the notes below.

Write **NO MORE THAN ONE WORD AND/OR A NUMBER** for each answer.

Camping and caravan park

Facilities:

- kitchen with dining area
- toilets and showers
- washing facilities
- **161** .... supply.

Open fires are allowed by the **162** ....

Reservations are advisable for big **163** ....

There is a non-refundable deposit of **164** £ ....

The rate per person: **165** £ .... per night.

The web page address is **166** www. .... .uk.com

The park closes at the end of **167** ....

You can arrive up to: **168** .... pm if booked online.

The distance to travel is more than: **169** .... miles.

Location is less than **170** .... metres from the postcode.

Section 2

Questions 171 to 177

Complete the table below.

Write **NO MORE THAN TWO WORDS AND/OR A NUMBER** for each answer.

TABLE 3.1

VOLUNTEERS WEEKEND				
Grade	Involves	Typical job	Fitness level	No of volunteers
1	**171**	clear Himalayan balsam, similar to **172**	low	**173** ....
2	moderate work	main job is **174**	**175**	2
3	heavy work	**176**	high	**177** ....

Questions 178 to 180

What does the speaker say about the following stones?

Write the correct letter, **A**, **B** or **C**, next to questions.

A	They are found in the middle of the wall.
B	They are mostly at the bottom of the wall.
C	They go right through the wall.

178 biggest stones ....

179 smallest stones ....

180 longest stones ....

Section 3

Questions 181 to 185

Choose the correct letter, **A**, **B** or **C**.

Work placements

181 Placements help students to

    A   see how a business operates.
    B   improve their business skills.
    C   write a business letter.

182 Graduates perform better at interviews because they

    A   have worked in the same place before.
    B   can speak confidently about the job.
    C   understand the work environment.

183 Students are expected to

    A   see things from the employer's perspective.
    B   improve their communication skills.
    C   work at an undergraduate level.

184 One advantage of work placements is that they

    A   tend to improve college work.
    B   are always positive experiences.
    C   separate theory from practice.

185 Difficulties in the workplace are sorted out by

    A   the students themselves.
    B   an academic member of staff.
    C   the mentor in the workplace.

Questions 186 to 190

Write the correct letter, **A**, **B** or **C**, next to the questions.

What does Mike say about the following work activities?

A　important to change.

B　hard to change.

C　possible to change.

186　poor timekeeping ....

187　dealing with problems ....

188　verbal and written skills ....

189　listening skills ....

190　being motivated ....

Section 4

Questions 191 to 200

Complete the notes below.

Write **NO MORE THAN ONE WORD OR ONE NUMBER** for each answer.

Darwin

Charles Darwin was born in 1809 in **191** ....

As a child, Darwin showed an interest in **192** .... , particularly insects.

Darwin attended medical school in 1825 but left in **193** ....

In 1831 Darwin left Plymouth, England, travelling by **194** ....

In 1835, he made important discoveries in the Galapagos Islands.

Darwin made sketches and **195** .... during the five-year voyage.

The results of the *Beagle* expedition were first published in **196** ....

In 1859, Darwin's famous book caused a great deal of **197** ....

Galapagos Islands

Spanish sailors have used Galapagos Island turtles for **198** ....

Darwin found fossils of creatures that had been unable to **199** ....

In Darwin's theory, nature selects which **200** .... will die out.

Reading (3)

Reading Passage 7

Recalling it

A Memory and recollection vary from person to person. Take three average citizens with a similar degree of honesty and integrity and ask them to make a statement concerning a bank raid that they all witnessed. Whilst the three statements will contain a fair degree of concurrence, there will also be areas of dissimilarity. When a person observes an event, not only are cognitive (or thinking) powers involved but also emotions are involved, especially when the incident observed is of an unpleasant nature.

B In our primitive ancestors, emotional stress had a survival value. It prepared us to face or flee a danger ('flight or fight' syndrome). Today's stressors are more likely to be perceived threats to an individual's well-being and self-esteem rather than actual threats to survival. However, any stressful situation, real or apparent, can trigger many of the same effects, for example, increased blood pressure, heart rate and anxiety.

C 'Pre-exam nerves' is an anxiety state experienced by candidates prior to an examination. It is perfectly natural to feel apprehensive about an important test. Negative thoughts disappear quickly when the candidate makes a promising start. On the other hand, a poor start increases the stress felt by the individual who can then experience a 'retrieval failure'. In this circumstance the information is held in the memory but cannot be accessed. The knowledge has been forgotten temporarily to remain on the 'tip-of the-tongue'. In intensely stressful situations, panic sets in and the relevant knowledge becomes blocked out completely by thoughts of failure.

D The ability to cope with stress is influenced by personality (way of thinking and behaving) and social circumstances, so what one person finds stressful another may find stimulating. Managing your own stress depends in part upon becoming aware of what your own particular stressors are. You can then confront each situation and try to change it and/or change your thoughts and emotional reactions to the stressor, so as to lessen its impact. Emotional support from family, friends and work colleagues leads to an improvement in coping with long-term stress. When confronted with a potentially stressful examination, one solution is to sit back, take a few deep breaths and relax to steady the nerves. Relaxation techniques will improve the memory but they cannot help a candidate to retrieve knowledge that they have yet to acquire. In this respect, short-term memory improves if you repeat new information to yourself several times, learning by rote.

E Clear and precise information is required when giving instructions. How often, in an unfamiliar district, has the reader stopped a passing stranger for simple and clear directions? How often also have the replies been unclear, rambling accompanied by wild gesticulations? The route may be clear in the eye of the director but the message is lost if salient points are either omitted or out of sequence. Accurate recall of past events is facilitated by note-taking and in particular by placing information under the headings: who, what, where, when and how. When information is classified under these headings it acts as a cue that enables the reader to construct partial images of previous events or to recall details that might otherwise be overlooked. It is important not to confuse facts with opinions and to clearly preface opinions with 'I believe', 'I think', 'In my view' or similar words. Memories can be triggered from several sources and it is useful to include both visual and verbal aids when revising for an examination. Revision tools include spider diagrams that expand on a central idea, coloured highlighting of related topics, flash cards with questions and answers, as well as mnemonic devices (small rhymes), such as 'I before e except after c', that aid spelling, for example.

F Nerves play a big part in public speaking. Despite this, an impromptu speech can be delivered effectively if the speaker is knowledgeable in the subject matter and sounds enthusiastic. Slide presentations are a popular means of delivering a speech. Typically, a 15-minute talk can be linked to a sequence of 30 slides, lasting 30 seconds on average. Each slide contains a few key elements that serve to cue the memory towards the necessary detail. It is essential to make a solid start, in which case it is advisable to memorize the opening lines of the speech by practising it out loud several times. The slides should link naturally so that the talk never sounds stilted. It is not necessary to memorize the speech word for word. All that is necessary is for the speaker to be familiar with the content of the slide and to develop the speech from the key words. It is advisable to record the speech on a dictaphone and then to play it back to check the continuity and duration.

Questions 201 to 205

Reading Passage 7 has six paragraphs, **A** to **F**.

Which paragraph contains the following information?

201 How early man benefited from stress.

202 How a person can reduce the effects of stress.

203 How candidates fear examinations.

204 How a speaker can make a confident start.

205 How communication fails if important facts are out of order.

Questions 206 to 210

Do the following statements agree with the information given in Reading Passage 7?

Write:

TRUE if the statement agrees with the information

FALSE if the statement contradicts the information

NOT GIVEN if there is no information on this.

206 Our primitive ancestors experienced higher levels of stress.

207 A 'retrieval failure' is a permanent loss of knowledge.

208 Learning by rote is memorizing by repetition.

209 Relaxation techniques can help a candidate to gain new knowledge.

210 Headings enable a complete image of an event to be recalled.

Questions 211 to 214

Choose the correct letter **A**, **B**, **C** or **D** for the questions based on Reading Passage 7.

211 To recall past events from notes it is helpful

    A   to place important points in sequence.

    B   to group information under headings.

    C   to construct partial images.

    D   to include a range of revision tools.

212 When revising for an examination it is helpful

    A   to use a range of memory aids.

    B   not to confuse facts with opinions.

    C   to include a slide presentation.

    D   to employ relaxation techniques.

213 A mnemonic is

    A   a verbal revision aid.

    B   an aural revision aid.

    C   a visual revision aid.

    D   a spelling revision aid.

214 A slide can help a speaker

    A   to make a confident start.

    B   to memorize a talk word for word.

    C   to recall essential information.

    D   to check the length of the speech.

Reading Passage 8

Home-schooling

A Introduction

In developed countries, compulsory education is the norm for children aged from around 6 to 16. Even so, in most cases this does not mean that the child has to attend a school. Increasing numbers of parents are choosing to educate their children at home. In the UK it is estimated that up to 100,000 pupils are being taught in this way, which equates to about 1% of the UK school population. In the USA, home education, or home schooling as it is known, has reached unprecedented levels with approximately 2 million children, or 4% of the compulsory age group, now receiving tuition at home. Parents cite various reasons for keeping their children away from school, ranging from a lack of satisfaction with the school environment to a wish to provide their own religious instruction. Home-schooling is a controversial issue surrounded by misgivings, with supporters emphasizing its benefits and detractors pointing to its limitations and risks.

B The reasons why parents elect to educate their children at home are often linked to emotionally charged issues rather than rational arguments that reflect the pros and cons of home-schooling. Typically, a child is removed from a school following negative experiences, for example bullying, or exposure to bad influences such as drugs, discrimination, bad language, or falling in with the wrong crowd. Consequently, home-schooling is ardently defended by its proponents who are not necessarily best placed to consider its downsides dispassionately. Whilst the popularity of home-education is on the increase, it remains an oddity, associated more with problems at school rather than a positive decision to provide a real alternative.

C Whilst home-schooling of a child is unusual, learning from parents is not, so formal teaching at home can be regarded as an extension of the parents' normal role. However, education in the home environment can have its limitations; for example, when there are gaps in the parents' knowledge in key subject areas such as fractions or algebra. Moreover, teaching is not merely the dispensing of knowledge acquired, but rather a skill that has to be taught, practised and mastered. Parents are not professional teachers and if the outcomes are poor then the parents can only blame themselves. Home-schooling is both time-consuming and demanding. Parents can lose out financially and socially when they are obliged to spend the entire day at home.

D Lack of socialization is perhaps the main criticism of home-schooling. When children are taken out of school they cannot interact with other pupils or engage in school activities, including team sports. Later, a young person may find it difficult to integrate in ordinary social settings or lack the coping skills to deal with the demands of everyday life. Socialization outside of the home can negate some of these short-comings, bearing in mind that the home-educated child is likely to have more free time to engage in recreational activities. Indeed, it might be argued that the socialization experienced in the natural setting of a community is preferable to that within the confines of a school.

E Whilst home-schooling has its shortcomings it also offers several advantages. Tuition is on a one-to-one basis so it can be personalized to meet an individual child's needs. There is no strict curriculum so the teaching can be readily adapted for those with special educational needs or learning disabilities. Children are allowed to develop at their own rate, and attention can be focussed on subjects that a child enjoys or has a particular aptitude for. Parents can provide religious education and impart moral values consistent with their own beliefs, and they can also include subjects that may not be available in their local schools, for example Latin or Archaeology. The timetable is entirely flexible with no time wasted travelling to and from school, no lack of educational continuity when moving home, and no restric-tions on when to take family holidays. It should come as no surprise that with all these benefits, home-educated children usually outperform their schooled counterparts academically. However, this is not conclusive proof of the effectiveness of home-schooling. Parents who home-school their children tend to be well-educated and in a higher than average income bracket. Consequently, these parents are more likely to show an interest in their child's education, encouraging compliance with home-work and offering support, meaning that the child would probably have performed well had they remained within the school system.

F Parents who educate their children at home may choose to shun school com-pletely. Despite this, local schools should offer parents and children support and guidance, extending access to school trips, library resources, recreational facilities, syllabus information, assessments and examinations. The future of home-schooling and its position in the education system are uncertain. Nevertheless, it is the duty of the state and the parents to ensure that home-educated children are given an education that affords them opportunities in life and equips them for the world of work.

Questions 215 to 219

Reading Passage 8 has six paragraphs, **A** to **F**.

Choose the correct heading for the paragraphs **B**, **C**, **D**, **E** and **F** from the list of headings below.

List of headings

i)	Disadvantages
ii)	Range of benefits
iii)	Problems at school
iv)	Main advantage
v)	Overcoming a weakness
vi)	No bad influences
vii)	Introduction
viii)	Shared responsibility
ix)	Parents as teachers

Paragraph **A** vii (Introduction)

215 Paragraph **B**

216 Paragraph **C**

217 Paragraph **D**

218 Paragraph **E**

219 Paragraph **F**.

Questions 220 to 226

Do the following statements agree with the information given in Reading Passage 8?

Write:

TRUE if the statement agrees with the information

FALSE if the statement contradicts the information

NOT GIVEN if there is no information on this.

220 In the USA there are four times as many home-educated children as in the UK.

221 There is much disagreement about the merits of home-schooling.

222 School children with disabilities are the most discriminated against.

223 There is nothing unusual about children learning from their parents at home.

224 Only children who attend school can be favourably socialized.

225 Pupils in school achieve higher grades than home-school children.

226 Children from better-off homes are more likely to complete their homework.

Reading Passage 9

Biofuels backlash

A Biodiesel and bio-ethanol are cleaner, sustainable alternatives to petroleum-based fuels, which continue to deplete. Biofuels can be grown repeatedly from crops making them 100% renewable. Bio-ethanol is made in a similar way to 'moonshine' by fermenting cereals like corn and maize and then distilling the brew to evaporate the ethanol. Biodiesel is manufactured from the vegetable oils found in sunflower seeds, rapeseed and the oil palm. Gasoline (petrol) engines can be tuned to run on 90% ethanol blended with 10% petroleum and biodiesel is a direct replacement for existing road diesel.

B Carbon-dioxide is the principal man-made greenhouse gas. It traps heat in the atmosphere and increases global warming, causing polar ice to recede and sea-levels to rise. Energy crops offer one solution to the deleterious effects of carbon-dioxide emitted from vehicle exhausts. Biofuels are 100% carbon-neutral, which means that there is no net gain or loss of carbon to the environment when the fuels are burnt. The carbon-dioxide does not add to the total amount in the atmosphere because the crops absorb the equivalent amount of carbon-dioxide by photosynthesis as they grow. Consequently, the 'carbon footprint' of gasoline- and diesel-powered vehicles can be reduced by switching to bio-ethanol or biodiesel. The latter burns more efficiently than petroleum diesel leaving less unburned hydrocarbons, carbon-monoxide and particulates, which means less atmospheric pollution as well as less global warming. Biofuels are less toxic than fossil fuels and biodegrade if spilt on the ground.

C Not everybody believes that biofuels are the ideal alternative to fossil fuels. The status of biofuels as environmentally friendly can be challenged on several counts. Firstly, to provide space for energy-crop plantations, trees are felled and burnt which creates a surplus of carbon-dioxide. Secondly, in tropical rainforests the loss of trees threatens biodiversity by destroying habitat. Thirdly, deforestation increases the evaporation of water from the ground, which can lead to extensive droughts. These deficits can be discounted if the energy crops are planted on existing agricultural land, but if this is done it reduces the supply of food crops, creating a surge in food prices. Furthermore, in developing countries people have barely sufficient food to eat and switching to fuel crops could threaten their meagre food supplies.

D To judge whether or not biofuels are genuinely a greener alternative to fossil fuels it is necessary to scrutinize the manufacturing steps. Whilst in theory, the carbon released by biofuels is equivalent to that removed from the atmosphere by the growing plants this does not reflect the true energy picture. Substantial amounts of nitrogen-based fertilizers are added to the soil to increase crop production. The process of manufacturing fertilizers consumes large amounts of energy in a process that burns natural gas and releases carbon-dioxide. What's more, when fertilizers are added to the land the soil releases nitrogen oxides into the atmosphere. As an agent of global warming, nitrous oxide is about 300 times more potent than carbon-dioxide, and surplus nitrates can leach into nearby rivers and streams where they kill the fish. The ethanol industry generates additional carbon-dioxide because many of its manufacturing plants use coal-fired boilers, and fossil fuels are also consumed by the vehicles that transport materials to and from manufacturing sites. Whilst the transportation of petroleum-based fuels also burns fossil fuels, biofuels are supposed to offer a greener alternative to the fuels they intend to replace.

E Biofuels may not be a panacea for global warning but they can play a part in a sustainable energy programme. To reinforce their green credentials, energy crops should not be planted on land that was being used to produce food. New technologies can produce ethanol from the inedible parts of plants, or from grasses grown on wasteland that is unsuitable for food. Genetically modified plants may be the answer to increasing biofuel crop yields without the need for further land grab. Plant strains can be developed that require little in the way of fertilizers or irrigation. Biodiesel consumption may, in the future, extend beyond transportation to include heating oils for domestic boilers. Developing countries that grow biofuels should be allowed to benefit from the premium prices that fuel crops command, enabling farmers and their communities to reap economic and social benefits. Whatever the advantages and disadvantages of fuel crops it is clear that fossil fuels are a limited resource and cannot remain the mainstay of our economies indefinitely.

Questions 227 to 231

Reading Passage 9 has five sections, **A** to **E**.

Choose the correct heading for the sections **A**, **B**, **C**, **D** and **E** from the list of headings below.

List of headings

i)   Biofuels

ii)   Fossil fuel replacements

iii) Advantages

iv)   The way forward

v)   Man made

vi)   Environmentally friendly

vii) Too much carbon

viii) Adverse effects

ix)   Unsustainable

x)   Thorough examination

---

227 Section A

228 Section B

229 Section C

230 Section D

231 Section E

Questions 232 to 236

Do the following statements agree with the information given in Reading Passage 9?

Write:

TRUE if the statement agrees with the information

FALSE if the statement contradicts the information

NOT GIVEN if there is no information on this.

232 Bio-ethanol is a non-renewable fuel source.

233 Burning biodiesel instead of petroleum diesel generates less pollution.

234 Food prices fall when fuel crops are planted on land used to grow food.

235 Fuel crops outnumber food crops in developing countries.

236 The eco-friendly nature of biofuels cannot be disputed.

Questions 237 to 240

Complete each sentence with the correct ending, **A** to **J**, below.

237 Excess fertilizer can be deadly to fish

238 The green status of energy crops is strengthened

239 It may not be necessary to acquire more land

240 Farmers in poorer countries will benefit from fuel crops

A if it is released from the soil into the atmosphere.

B when they play a part in a sustainable energy programme.

C if they are not planted on agricultural land.

D if they are planted on land used to produce food.

E if nitrogen-based fertilizers are added to the soil.

F when new technologies are employed.

G if it drains into the surrounding watercourses.

H if they can keep the profits they make.

I when fossil fuels eventually run out.

J if yields are improved with genetically modified crops.

Writing (3)

Writing task 1

You should spend about 20 minutes on this task.

The table below gives information on internet use in six categories by age group.

Describe the information in the table and make comparisons where appropriate.

Write at least 150 words.

Internet activities by age group

TABLE 3.2

Percentage %	Age groups						
	Teens	**20s**	**30s**	**40s**	**50s**	**60s**	**70+**
Use e-mail	90	91	93	94	95	90	91
Online games	80	55	36	25	20	27	29
Download music and videos	52	46	27	15	13	8	6
Travel reservations	0	51	74	65	60	58	61
Online purchase	39	67	69	67	65	64	40
Searching for people	3	30	33	26	25	27	31

Writing task 2

You should spend about 40 minutes on this task.

Is fast food to blame for obesity in society or is gaining too much weight the responsibility of the individual?

What factors contribute to obesity?

Why do you think that children are becoming obese?

Give reasons for your answer and include any relevant experience or knowledge.

Write at least 250 words.

Speaking (3)

Part 1 Familiar topics

Pets

Do you or your family own any pets?

- Who looks after your pet? [Why?]
  My neighbour looks (present tense) after my ....

- Why did you choose this pet?
  I chose (past tense) a dog because ....

- Is it expensive to keep your pet? [Why? Why not?]
  No it's not (present tense) expensive unless I have to take (present tense)
  it to see the vet in which case ....

- Is it looked after carefully? [How?]
  I've always looked (past tense) after all the pets I've had (past tense) and my
  dog is (present tense) important to me, so ....

Part 2 Brief talk

I want you to talk about a topic I'm going to give you. You have one minute to think
about what you are going to say. You can make some notes to help you. Your talk
should last between one and two minutes.

Talk about a holiday/vacation you remember well.

[Where did you go?] [Who did you go with?]

[Did you fly?] [Did you stay in a hotel?]

[What was the weather like?]

[How did you spend your time?]

How did it compare with other holidays?

Part 3 Discussion

Work and play

Should people work fewer hours and have longer holidays?

Can you spend less time working but get more things done? [Why?/Why not?]

Do you think that you can take more leisure time and still be successful? [How?]

Why is it difficult to work fewer hours?

Is it important to balance work time and family time? [Why? How?]

Tip: if you don't understand the question it is OK to ask the interviewer to repeat it. There are no right or wrong answers in the speaking section.

TEST 4

Listening (4)

Section 1

Questions 241 to 245

Complete the notes below.

Write **NO MORE THAN THREE WORDS AND/OR A NUMBER** for each answer.

Library registration

Student requires proof of identity and proof of **241** ....

Documents checked:

- Passport ✓
- Drivers licence
- Utility contract
- **242** landlord's .... ✓
- Other

PIN must be a **243** ....

E-mail address for:

- Reserves
- Overdue items
- Information on **244** ....

The library card number is below the **245** ....

Questions 246 to 250

Complete the form below.

Write **NO MORE THAN TWO WORDS AND/OR A NUMBER** for each answer.

Library policy

Maximum number of items that can be borrowed is **246** ....

Loan periods:

- Books: normally 3 weeks
- New releases: **247** ....
- Magazines: 10 days ....
- DVDs and CDs: **248** ....

Renewals: made online, in person or by phone.

Reserved items need to be collected within **249** ....

Students cannot reserve **250** ....

Section 2

Questions 251 to 257

Choose the correct letter, **A**, **B** or **C**.

Travelling by train

251 The train to Telstar city leaves at

    A 15.05 hours.
    B 15.15 hours.
    C 15.50 hours.

252 Boarding passes are available near

    A the main gate.
    B the main entrance.
    C the main hall.

253 Ticket machines can be found

    A at the green booth.
    B in the main hall.
    C on the platform.

254 Passengers who paid for their tickets online can access the platform via

    A gate B.
    B gate P.
    C gate T.

255 Boarding will start at around

    A 15.05 hours.
    B 15.09 hours.
    C 15.50 hours.

256 Passengers should board either

    A standard or first class.
    B standard or premium class.
    C ordinary or luxury class.

257 Reserved seats will not be held after

    A   15.40 hours.

    B   15.30 hours.

    C   15.20 hours.

Questions 258 to 260

Complete the table below.

Write **NO MORE THAN THREE WORDS** for each answer.

TABLE 4.1

Class	Remarks
Standard	Small choice of **258** ....
Premium	Free **259** ....
Sleeper	As premium plus free **260** ....

Section 3

Questions 261 to 265

Choose the correct letter, **A**, **B** or **C**.

Home composting

261 What is the main reason for the current interest in home composting?

    A a lack of landfill space.

    B to reduce greenhouse emissions.

    C it improves the soil.

262 Dr Rotenberg says that landfill sites lead to

    A confusion about composting.

    B increased transportation costs.

    C more emissions from vehicles.

263 Home composting reduces greenhouse gases because

    A there is enough oxygen.

    B there are enough bacteria.

    C there is enough heat.

264 Dr Rotenberg describes organic material as

    A mainly carbon.

    B living.

    C greens and browns.

265 Composting usually requires brown materials to be

    A mixed together with green materials.

    B placed on top of green materials.

    C kept separate from green materials.

Questions 266 to 270

Complete the diagram below.

Write **ONE WORD/NUMBER ONLY** for each answer.

Home composter

Composter made from
266 ....
or recyclable plastic
Holds compost for up to
267 .... months
Container with a
268 ....
for kitchen scraps
Enclosure in the garden to hold
269 ....
Shredded card or screwed up
270 ....
improve the airflow

Section 4

Questions 271 to 280

Complete the notes below.

Write **ONE WORD ONLY** for each answer.

Academic essays

Page set-up

- Do not change the standard **271** ....

- Double spaced for the tutor's remarks and to help with **272** ....

Text

- Font should be 12 point Times New Roman.

- The essay must not be **273** ....

Marking

- The marker knows the candidate's **274** .... only.

- If you write too much it might not be **275** .... by the examiner.

Referencing

- Some researchers might want to find the **276** .... of the information.

- There is no need to reference **277** .... that are common knowledge.

- Do not quote the author's **278** .... name in the main text.

- The **279** .... of references need to be alphabetized.

- The place of and the name of the publisher come **280** ....

Reading (4)

Reading Passage 10

Hacked off

Internet security, or rather the lack of it, is the bane of today's computer user. Computer hackers write malicious computer programs (or malware) that infect vulnerable computers and modify the way they operate. Typically, these programs are downloaded from the internet inadvertently with a single click of the mouse. The consequences are detrimental to the user, ranging from a minor nuisance – for example, slowing the computer's speed – to a major financial loss for an individual or company, when login and password details are accessed and fraud ensues. Examples of malware include viruses, worms, trojans (Trojan horses), spyware, keystroke logging, scareware and dishonest adware.

A virus can be released when a user opens an e-mail and downloads an attachment. The text portion of the e-mail cannot carry any malware but the attachment may contain a virus, for example in a macro (a short program) embedded in a worksheet document, such as Excel. Viruses can replicate and if they spread to the host computer's boot sector files they can leave the user with a 'blue-screen of death'. In this circumstance, the blue-screen is accompanied by a message that starts 'A problem has been detected and Windows has been shut down to prevent damage to your computer'. Whilst malware cannot physically damage the computer's hard drive the information on the boot sector has been destroyed and the computer is unable to function. In a worst case scenario the hard disk has to be wiped clean by reformatting, before the operating system can be reinstalled, in which case every program and file will be lost.

Unlike a virus, a worm can infect a computer without the user downloading an attachment, so it can spread through a network of computers at tremendous speed. The ability of worms to replicate in this way means that they can infect every contact in the user's e-mail address book and potentially every e-mail contact in each recipient's computer. Instant messaging programs and social networking sites are similarly at risk. A main feature of a worm is that it slows the computer down by consuming memory or hard disk space so that the computer eventually locks up.

The word trojan derives from the Trojan Horse of Greek mythology that tricked the Trojans into allowing Greek soldiers into the city of Troy, hidden inside a wooden horse. Today a trojan is a metaphor for malware that masquerades as useful software.

Trojans are unable to replicate but they interfere with the computer surreptitiously, allowing viruses and worms unfettered access to the system.

Spyware programs monitor a computer user's internet surfing habits covertly. Some spyware simply monitors how many visits consumers make to particular web pages and what they are buying or spending, usually for marketing purposes. Keystroke logging is the main fraudulent activity linked to spyware. Here, private and confidential information is obtained from the user's keystrokes, enabling criminals to acquire credit card details, or login names and passwords for online bank accounts. Some keystroke loggers operate legitimately to monitor the internet use of employees in the office or to keep tabs on children's surfing activities at home.

Scareware is a form of extortion where a victim is informed that the computer is infected with a virus and, for a fee, is offered a solution to fix the problem. The user is tricked into clicking an 'OK' button and buys software unnecessarily because there is usually no virus. In one scam, a scareware pop-up informs the victim that the computer's registry contains critical errors when the problems are actually minor or even non-existent. Persuaded by the pop-up advert, the victim buys the 'registry cleaner', which may not work or could even damage the computer's registry. There are of course legitimate registry cleaners that will boost your computer's speed. A genuine registry cleaner will normally be endorsed by a reputable company or recommended in a PC magazine.

Adware pop-up adverts are similar to scareware but are merely a nuisance rather than malware (unless dishonest), though they can still download programs that track your shopping habits and slow your computer down. The adverts pop up automatically when the user opens the internet browser and can become irritating because they conceal information on the opened up page. One answer is to turn on the Internet Explorer's pop-up blocker under the privacy tab because this will block most automatic pop-ups. More effectively, a user can purchase an all-in-one security suite to block any malware. Security software automatically blocks and deletes any malicious programs for a more secure web experience. Normally, the software will update itself every day as long as the computer is switched on.

Questions 281 to 287

Do the following statements agree with the information given in Reading Passage 10?

Write:

TRUE if the statement agrees with the information

FALSE if the statement contradicts the information

NOT GIVEN if there is no information on this.

281 Malware is usually downloaded from the internet by mistake.

282 An e-mail text can carry a virus.

283 A virus can result in the loss of every program and file.

284 Java applets can contain malicious code.

285 A Trojan disguises itself as useful software.

286 Keystroke logging is always fraudulent.

287 Scareware is not harmful to the user.

Questions 288 to 292

Classify the following as typical of

    A   a virus

    B   a worm

    C   a virus and a worm.

288 requires user input to infect a computer.

289 can duplicate itself.

290 reduces the computer's speed.

291 do not damage the hard drive.

292 can be removed by security software.

Reading Passage 11

Highlands and Islands

A Off the west coast of Scotland, in the Atlantic Ocean, lies a chain of islands known as the Outer Hebrides or Western Isles. The main inhabited islands are Lewis, Harris, North Uist and South Uist, Benbecula, Berneray and Barra. The Isle of Lewis is the most northern and largest of the Western Isles, and to its south, a small strip of land connects it to the Isle of Harris, making the two islands one land mass. To the south west of Harris are the two Uists with Benbecula wedged in between them. These three islands are connected by bridges and causeways. The small island of Berneray is connected to North Uist by a causeway and it is the only populated island in the waters around Harris. Eriskay is a tiny island, also populated, lying between South Uist and Barra. Off the tip of Barra lie the Barra Isles, formerly known as the Bishop's Isles, comprising a group of small islands which include Mingulay, Sandray, Pabbay and Vatersay, and at the southernmost tip of the chain, lies an island by the name of Berneray, not to be confused with the island of the same name observed across the bay from Harris.

B Lewis is low-lying and covered in a smooth blanket of peatland. Harris is an island of contrasts. It displays a rocky coast to the east, yet white, sandy beaches to the west, backed by fertile green grassland ('machair'), pockmarked with freshwater pools (lochans). North Uist is covered with peatland and lochans, whilst South Uist is mountainous to the east with machair and sandy beaches to the west. Benbecula is relatively flat and combines machair, peatland and lochans, with sandy beaches and deeply indented sea lochs. Like Harris, Benbecula and Barra exhibit a rocky coast-land to the east and low-lying machair to the west with sandy beaches similar to those seen on Berneray, which is a flat isle, except for a few hills, and sand dunes.

C Although part of Scotland, the Western Isles have a distinctive culture. Whilst English is the dominant language of mainland Scotland, Gaelic is the first language of more than half the islanders, and visitors to the islands can expect a Gaelic greeting. Gaelic signing and labelling reinforces the unique identity of the islands and helps to promote tourism and business. Place names on road signs are in Gaelic with only the main signs displaying English beneath. Visitors to the Western Isles may be surprised to find that the shops are closed on Sundays. The strong Christian tradition of the islands means that for the most part, the Sabbath is respected as a day of rest and leisure, especially on Lewis and Harris.

D There are approximately 27,000 people in the Western Isles and one-third of these live in and around the capital town of Stornoway, on the east coast of the Isle of Lewis. The town is served by an airport and ferry terminal making it the hub for Western Islands' travel. Stornoway is best known for its world-famous Harris Tweed industry, which developed from a Murray tartan commissioned by Lady Dunmore in the 1850s. Only wool that has been hand-woven and dyed in the Outer Hebrides is permitted to carry the Harris Tweed logo. Other areas of economic activity include fishing, tourism, transport and renewable energy. Almost two-thirds of the population live on a croft, which is a particular type of smallholding peculiar to the Highlands and Islands of Scotland. Crofters are tenants of a small piece of agricultural land, typically a few hectares, that usually includes a dwelling which the crofter either owns or rents from the landowner. The land must be used for the purposes of crofting, which can be described as small-scale mixed farming. Crofting activities include grazing sheep (lamb) and to lesser extent cattle (beef), growing potatoes, vegetables and fruit, keeping chickens, and cutting peat for burning on the house fire. Crofting can be likened to subsistence living, that is to say, living off what you can rear, grow and make, with anything spare going to market or shared with the community. Some people see crofting as a means of escaping the 'rat race' and getting closer to nature, though this romanticized view is naive. It is difficult to survive from crofting alone and most crofters have to supplement their incomes with a part-time job. Crofting as a way of life has been in decline. However, this trend may be about to reverse, led by consumer demand for high-quality produce, grown sustainably with the least environmental impact.

Questions 293 to 299

Do the following statements agree with the information given in Reading Passage 11?

Write:

TRUE if the statement agrees with the information

FALSE if the statement contradicts the information

NOT GIVEN if there is no information on this.

293 The Isles of Lewis and Harris are joined together.

294 There are two islands called Berneray in the sea around Harris.

295 The sea around Benbecula is deep.

296 On the island of South Uist, there are fertile green grasslands and sandy beaches to the west and many islanders can speak Gaelic.

297 In the Western Isles most road signs are bilingual.

298 Approximately 9,000 people live in or near Stornoway.

299 Most crofters earn their living entirely from crofting.

Questions 300 to 302

The passage described the position of the islands in relation to each other. There are four unnamed islands, **A**, **B**, **C** and **D** on the map below.

Complete the table below.

TABLE 4.2

Name of Island	Label A, B, C or D
Lewis	**300**
Eriskay	**301**
Berneray	**302**

Map of the Western Isles

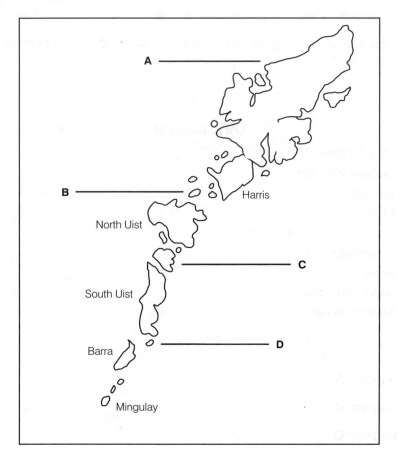

A ——————————

B ——————————

Harris

North Uist

C ——————————

South Uist

D ——————————

Barra

Mingulay

Questions 303 to 306

Reading Passage 11 has four paragraphs, **A** to **D**.

Choose the correct heading for the paragraphs **A**, **B**, **C** and **D** from the list of headings below.

List of headings

i)	Life in the Western Isles
ii)	Language and culture
iii)	Environment
iv)	Landscape
v)	Population and economic activity
vi)	Sustainability
vii)	Location
viii)	History and heritage
ix)	Travel and tourism

---

303 Paragraph **A**

304 Paragraph **B**

305 Paragraph **C**

306 Paragraph **D**

Reading Passage 12

Dummy pills

There is an ongoing debate about the merits and the ethics of using placebos, sometimes called 'sugar pills'. The 'placebo effect' is well documented though not completely understood. It refers to the apparent benefits, both psychological and physiological, of taking a medication or receiving a treatment that you expect will improve your health, when in fact the tablet contains no active ingredients and the treatment has never been proven. Any benefit that arises from a placebo originates solely in the mind of the person taking it. The therapeutic effect can be either real and measurable or perceived and imagined.

The placebo effect is a headache for drug manufactures. 'Guinea pig' patients, that is to say, those who volunteer for a new treatment, may show positive health gains from the placebo effect that masks the response to the treatment. This has led to the introduction of double-blind trials – experiments where neither the patient nor the healthcare professional observing the patient knows whether a placebo has been used or not. So, for example, in a 'randomized control trial' (RCT), patients are selected at random and half the patients are given the new medication and half are given a placebo tablet that looks just the same. The observer is also 'blind' to the treatment to avoid bias. If the observer knows which patients are receiving the 'real' treatment they may be tempted to look harder for greater health improvements in these people in comparison with those on the placebo.

Whilst the case for placebos in drug trials appears to be justified, there are ethical issues to consider when using placebos. In particular, the need to discontinue placebos in clinical trials in favour of 'real' medication that is found to work, and whether a placebo should ever be prescribed in place of a real treatment without the patient ever knowing. In the first circumstance, it would be unethical to deny patients a new and effective treatment in a clinical trial and also unethical to stop patients from taking their existing tablets so that they can enter a trial. These two ethical perspectives are easy to understand. What is perhaps less clear is the distinction between a placebo that may have therapeutic value and a 'quack cure' which makes claims without any supporting evidence.

Quackery was at its height at the end of the nineteenth century, when so-called men of medicine peddled fake remedies claiming that all manner of diseases and afflictions could be cured. The modern equivalent of these quack cures are 'complementary and alternative medicine' (CAM) which are unable to substantiate the claims they make. There are dozens of these treatments, though the best-known are perhaps acupuncture, homeopathy, osteopathy and reflexology. There is anecdotal evidence from patients that these treatments are effective but no scientific basis to support the evidence. Whilst recipients of complementary and alternative medicine (CAM) can find the treatment to be therapeutic, it is not possible to distinguish these benefits from the placebo effect. Consequently it is important not to turn to alternative therapies too early but to adhere to modern scientific treatments. Complementary therapies are by definition intended to be used alongside traditional medicine as an adjunct treatment to obtain, at the very least, a placebo effect. With either complementary or alternative therapies the patient may notice an improvement in their health and link it with the therapy, when in fact it is the psychological benefit derived from a bit of pampering in a relaxing environment that has led to feelings of improvement, or it could be nature taking its course.

Patients enter into a clinical trial in the full knowledge that they have a 50/50 chance of receiving the new drug or the placebo. An ethical dilemma arises when a placebo is considered as a treatment in its own right; for example, in patients whose problems appear to be 'all in the mind'. Whilst a placebo is by definition harmless and the 'placebo effect' is normally therapeutic, the practice is ethically dubious because the patient is being deceived into believing that the treatment is authentic. The person prescribing the placebo may hold the view that the treatment can be justified as long as it leads to an improvement in the patient's health. However, benevolent efforts of this type are based on a deception that could, if it came to light, jeopardize the relationship between the physician and the patient. It is a small step between prescribing a placebo and believing that the physician always knows best, thereby denying patients the right to judge for themselves what is best for their own bodies. Whilst it is entirely proper for healthcare professionals to act at all times in patients' best interests, honesty is usually the best policy where medical treatments are concerned, in which case dummy pills have no place in modern medicine outside of clinical trials. On the other hand, complementary medicine, whilst lacking scientific foundations, should not be considered unethical if it is able to demonstrate therapeutic benefits, even if only a placebo effect, as long as patients are not given false hopes nor hold unrealistic expectations, and are aware that the treatment remains unproven.

Questions 307 to 310

Choose the correct letter **A**, **B**, **C** or **D** for the questions based on Reading Passage 12.

307 The passage 'Dummy pills' is mainly concerned with

  A real and imagined treatments.
  B the use of complementary and alternative medicine (CAM).
  C the value and morality of placebo use.
  D alternatives to traditional medicine.

308 In the passage, the author states that the action of a placebo

  A is entirely understood.
  B is based on the patient's expectations of success.
  C is based on the active ingredients in the tablet.
  D is entirely psychological.

309 The author suggests that in volunteers, the placebo effect

  A may hide the effect of the drug being tested.
  B makes positive health gains a certainty.
  C is random response to a new treatment.
  D causes bias in double-blind experiments.

310 The author states that it is morally wrong for patients to use placebos

  A in clinical drug trials.
  B if they do not know that they are taking them.
  C without any supporting evidence.
  D instead of their current treatment.

Questions 311 to 316

Do the following statements agree with the information given in Reading Passage 12?

Write:

TRUE if the statement agrees with the information

FALSE if the statement contradicts the information

NOT GIVEN if there is no information on this.

311 The author states that quack cures can be likened to complementary and alternative medicine (CAM).

312 There are personal accounts of complementary and alternative medicine being successful.

313 Complementary medicine should be used separately from traditional medicine.

314 Health improvements following complementary or alternative therapies may not have been caused by the therapies.

315 People turn to complementary and alternative therapies too early.

316 There can be risks associated with alternative therapies.

Questions 317 to 320

Complete the summary using the list of words, **A** to **K**, below.

Patients in a clinical trial are fully aware that they have only a 50% chance of receiving the new drug. Even so, prescribing a placebo as a treatment presents the physician with a moral **317** .... Even if the treatment works, the patient has been tricked into believing that the placebo was **318** .... and if this were found out it could **319** .... the physician–patient relationship. Furthermore, patients should not be denied the right to make **320** .... about their own treatment.

A genuine	**B** deception	**C** belief	**D** questions	**E** correct	**F** harm
G improve	**H** dilemma	**I** story	**J** choices	**K** ethical

Writing (4)

Writing task 1

You should spend about 20 minutes on this task.

The bar chart shows different methods of waste disposal in four towns, named A, B, C and D.

Summarize the information by describing the main features of the chart and making comparisons where appropriate.

Write at least 150 words.

Waste disposal in four towns

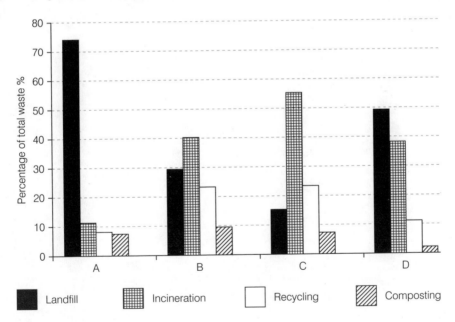

Writing task 2

You should spend about 40 minutes on this task.

Do good exam results at school or college guarantee success in life?

Discuss the advantages that a good education can have on your future.

Do you believe that studying hard will bring a better life?

Give reasons for your answer and include any relevant experience or knowledge.

Write at least 250 words.

Speaking (4)

Part 1 Familiar topics

Educational achievement

- What are your academic qualifications?
  I have (present tense) a degree in . . . .

- Why did you choose this subject?
  I chose (past tense) psychology because . . . .

- Which subjects do you like the most? [Why?]
  Mostly I like (present tense) . . . .

- Which subject do you find the most difficult? [Why?]
  I find (present tense) . . . .

Part 2 Brief talk

I want you to talk about a topic I'm going to give you. You have one minute to think about what you are going to say. You can make some notes to help you. Your talk should last between one and two minutes.

Describe a book that you have read this year.

[What type of book was it?] [What was the subject?] [Why did you choose this book?]
[How big was it?] [How long did it take to read?] [Was it a good book?]

Would you recommend the book to a friend?

Part 3 Discussion

Reading books

Do you think that children spend enough time reading books? [Why?/Why not?]

Should parents read books to children at bedtime? [Why?]

What are the advantages of reading books?

Which is more useful: reading a book or watching a film?

Tip: Speak as clearly as you can and try to find the right words. The interviewer will be listening for your range of vocabulary and the accuracy of your grammar.

General Reading and Writing Test A

General Training Reading

Test A

Section 1

Questions 321 to 335

Read the text below and answer questions 321 to 327.

Check-in procedure at Stanza airport

Check-in

The flight desk opens 2 hours before the scheduled departure time. The latest check-in is 45 minutes before departure. Passengers must deposit their hold baggage at the flight desk where they will be issued with a boarding pass and a seat number.

Identification

Passengers will need:

- Valid passport or photo ID.
- Valid airline ticket or reservation code.

Baggage weight allowance

- Economy Class: 18 kg of hold allowance included in the ticket.
- Business Class: 24 kg of hold allowance included in the ticket.
- Excess baggage charges are £5 per kg up to a maximum weight of 28 kg.

If your hold baggage exceeds the maximum weight of 28 kg you must switch some items to your hand luggage.

Hand luggage (cabin baggage)

- Hand luggage: Passengers are restricted to one piece of cabin luggage with a maximum weight of 8 kg and a maximum size of 50 cm x 40 cm x 20 cm.

Security restrictions

- NO sharp items such as knives or scissors are to be carried in hand luggage.
- NO flammable liquids, compressed gases, hazardous chemicals or explosive substances under any circumstances.
- Liquids, gels and pastes (drink, shampoo, toothpaste, etc): individual containers must not exceed 100 ml (3.5 fl oz). All items must be kept in a single, transparent, plastic bag, approximately 20 cm × 20 cm, knotted or tied at the top, which holds no more than 1 litre. All items of hand luggage will be screened by x-ray.

Questions 321 to 327

Do the following statements agree with the information given in the text?

Write:

TRUE if the statement agrees with the information

FALSE if the statement contradicts the information

NOT GIVEN if there is no information on this.

321 Passengers must leave their hand luggage (cabin baggage) at the flight desk no later than 45 minutes before departure.

322 Passengers must have some means of photo identification.

323 Passengers must have both the correct ticket and the reservation code.

324 There is no charge for 18 kg of hold baggage.

325 Passengers may pre-book an additional 28 kg of hold luggage.

326 Passengers with breathing problems can take compressed oxygen on-board.

327 Toiletries must be placed together in a clear plastic bag.

Read the text below and answer Questions 328 to 334.

You're fired!

'Employment at will'

In the USA, employment is typically on an 'at will' basis, meaning that your employer can fire you 'at will' for whatever reason. Being late for work at an at-will firm could cost you your job without any warning, period of notice, or legal rights to fight the decision. Whilst this behaviour appears harsh, it allows employers to dismiss lazy or incompetent people easily and then hire new people to take their place. 'Employment at will' means no contract of employment and no job security.

'Just cause'

Not all US firms are 'at-will' employers. Some workers have to sign a contract that sets out the employee's terms and conditions (for example, pay, annual leave and rest periods). If an employer wishes to terminate the contract they must provide the employee at least 30 days' notice in advance, or pay 30 days' wages in lieu of the period of notice. Employers are expected to adhere to any dismissal procedures set out in the employee's handbook. Typically this means that you cannot be fired for bad timekeeping without receiving prior verbal and written warnings. If you fail to heed a written warning, and continue to arrive late for work, then your employer has 'just cause' to dismiss you.

'Sacked'

In the UK there is no such thing as 'employment at will'. In UK employment law there is always a contract between an employer and an employee whether or not it is written down. An employee cannot be dismissed without 'just cause'. However, an employee can be dismissed immediately for gross misconduct such as theft, indecent behaviour, or drinking alcohol on duty. The colloquial term for dismissal in the UK is 'sacked', though the term 'fired' is widely understood. An employee has no rights to 30 days' notice or 30 days' wages in lieu of the notice period when they have been sacked due to gross misconduct.

Questions 328 to 334

Complete the sentences below.

Choose **NO MORE THAN TWO WORDS** from the passage for each answer.

328 You can be fired for any .... if you are 'employed at will'.

329 Thirty days' .... can be paid instead of advanced notice.

330 Information on .... is contained in the employee's handbook.

331 An employer has .... to terminate your contract if you have failed to observe a written warning.

332 In UK law, a contract of employment does not have to be ....

333 Theft and drinking alcohol on duty are examples of ....

334 In the UK, people are described as having been .... rather than fired.

Section 2

Questions 335 to 340

Read the text below and answer Questions 335 to 340.

NEWVIEW HOTEL
TERMS AND CONDITIONS

Bookings
Guests may book via the website or on arrival. Rooms are subject to availability and the management reserves the right to refuse a booking if your accommodation is no longer available for reasons beyond our control.

Charges
The prices displayed on the website are the total for your requested stay and are inclusive of breakfast (served from 08.15 to 09.30). Extras such as evening meals and drinks are additional.

Payment
A non-refundable deposit equal to 100% of the cost of the first night's booking is required with any reservation. The balance of the booking is paid on departure. Bookings made on a special discounted rate require full prepayment for the entire booking at the time of the booking, and are non-refundable and non-transferable. Payment can be made by credit or debit card. All payments made by credit card will attract a 2% surcharge.

Cancellations
If a booking is cancelled with at least 48 hours' warning there will not be a charge other than the deposit. Bookings that are cancelled with less than 48 hours' warning, or by way of a 'no-show', will incur the cost of the entire reservation. We recommend that you take out a holiday cancellation insurance policy that covers cancellations through accidents and illness.

Arrival and departure
Guests may check in at any time from 15.00 hrs on the day of arrival. An early check-in is available from 11.00 hrs for an extra charge of £5. All guests are requested to vacate their rooms by 11.00 hrs on the day of departure. A late check out is available up to 14.00 hrs for an extra charge of £10.

Breakages/losses
We do not normally charge for minor breakages but may do so where the damages or breakages are significant. The agent responsible for the booking will be debited with the costs.
   A fee of £10 will be charged to the room holder for keys that are lost or not returned.

Parking
There is plenty of free parking at the rear of the hotel. The management does not accept liability for loss or damage to vehicles unless caused by ourselves.

Questions 335 to 340

Answer the questions below.

Choose **NO MORE THAN THREE WORDS AND/OR A NUMBER** from the text for each answer.

335 How can guests make a reservation before they arrive?

336 Which meal incurs no extra charge?

337 How much of the first night's booking is paid in advance?

338 What cost is incurred for a cancellation made before the booking date?

339 What is the latest time that a guest can vacate their room on departure?

340 Who pays for replacement keys?

Questions 341 to 347

Read the text below and answer Questions 341 to 347.

A Proper Brew
EIGHT STEPS TO A PERFECT CUP OF TEA

1   Empty the old water out of the kettle and fill it up with fresh water from the cold water tap. In some hard-water areas it may be necessary to use filtered water. Do not fill the kettle with more water than you need because this wastes energy. Switch the kettle on to boil.

2   Meanwhile get out the following items: teapot; tea cosy if you have one; teapot stand; milk; white sugar or sweeteners; and the required number of mugs or cups.

3   When the kettle is hot, but not yet boiling, add some water to the teapot to preheat it, and then pour this water away. Do not wait until the kettle is boiling before preheating the teapot because the water will need to be boiled again and this wastes energy. A cold teapot absorbs some of the heat needed for the brewing process.

4   Place the tea bags in the warmed teapot. One tea bag per person will make a strong brew. Two tea bags, properly infused, are sufficient to make three cups of tea with the correct amount of water in the teapot.

5   When the water comes to the boil, pour it onto the tea bags and give the brew a quick stir. Place the lid on the pot and put on the tea cosy to keep the brew warm. A teapot stand will protect the work surface from the heat of the pot.

6   Allow the tea to infuse for between three and five minutes to achieve the desired strength, according to taste. If you prefer black tea, then two minutes might be sufficient, whereas a herbal or fruit tea might need at least six minutes.

7   Pour a small amount of milk into the empty cups or mugs, and add the desired amount of sugar if required. Alternatively you can wait until the tea has been poured out before adding the milk and sugar, if you prefer.

8   Remove the tea cosy and pour the tea into the cups. Biscuits are an optional extra. Digestives and Rich-tea biscuits are ideal for dunking.

Questions 341 to 347

Complete the sentences below.

Choose **NO MORE THAN TWO WORDS** from the text for each answer.

341 Some people fill the kettle with too much water, which ....

342 Before the kettle boils you can .... the cups.

343 Preheating the teapot helps with the ....

344 It is possible to make three cups of tea from two tea bags ....

345 The heat of the pot can damage the ....

346 Black tea can reach the .... after two minutes.

347 Some people .... to add milk and sugar last.

Section 3

Questions 348 to 360

Read the passage and answer Questions 348 to 360.

Vertical transport

A DEATH DEFYING STUNT THAT SHAPED THE SKYLINE OF THE WORLD

A The raising of water from a well using a bucket suspended from a rope can be traced back to ancient times. If the rope was passed over a pulley wheel it made the lifting less strenuous. The method could be improved upon by attaching an empty bucket to the opposite end of the rope, then lowering it down the well as the full bucket came up, to counterbalance the weight.

B Some medieval monasteries were perched on the tops of cliffs that could not be readily scaled. To overcome the problem, a basket was lowered to the base of the cliff on the end of a rope coiled round a wooden rod, known as a windlass. It was possible to lift heavy weights with a windlass, especially if a small cog wheel on the cranking handle drove a larger cog wheel on a second rod. Materials and people were hoisted in this fashion, but it was a slow process and if the rope were to break the basket plummeted to the ground.

C In the middle of the nineteenth century the general public considered elevators supported by a rope to be too dangerous for personal use. Without an elevator, the height of a commercial building was limited by the number of steps people could be expected to climb within an economic time period. It was the American inventor and manufacturer Elisha Graves Otis (1811–61) who finally solved the problem of passenger elevators.

D In 1852, Otis pioneered the idea of a safety brake, and two years later he demonstrated it in spectacular fashion at the New York Crystal Palace Exhibition of Industry. Otis stood on the lifting platform, four storeys above an expectant crowd. The rope was cut, and after a small jolt, the platform came to a halt. Otis' stunt increased people's confidence in elevators and sales increased.

E The operating principle of the safety elevator was described and illustrated in its pattern documentation of 1861. The lifting platform was suspended between two vertical posts each lined with a toothed guide rail. A hook was set into the sides of the platform to engage with the teeth, allowing movement vertically upwards but not downwards. Descent of the elevator was possible only if the hooks were pulled in, which could only happen when the rope was in tension. If the rope were to break, the tension would be lost and the hooks would spring outwards to engage the teeth and stop the fall. Modern elevators incorporate similar safety mechanisms.

F Otis installed the first passenger elevator in a store in New York City in 1957. Following the success of the elevator, taller buildings were constructed, and sales increased once more as the business expanded into Europe. England's first Otis passenger elevator (or lift as the British say) appeared four years later with the opening of London's Grosvenor Hotel. Today, the Otis Elevator Company continues to be the world's leading manufacturer of elevators, employing over 60,000 people with markets in 200 countries. More significantly perhaps, the advent of passenger lifts marked the birth of the modern skyscraper.

G Passenger elevators were powered by steam prior to 1902. A rope carrying the cab was wound round a revolving drum driven by a steam engine. The method was too slow for a tall building, which needed a large drum to hold a long coil of rope. By the following year, Otis had developed a compact electric traction elevator that used a cable but did away with the winding gear, allowing the passenger cab to be raised over 100 storeys both quickly and efficiently.

H In the electric elevator, the cable was routed from the top of the passenger cab to a pulley wheel at the head of the lift shaft and then back down to a weight acting as a counterbalance. A geared-down electric motor rotated the pulley wheel, which contained a groove to grip the cable and provide the traction. Following the success of the electric elevator, skyscraper buildings began to spring up in the major cities. The Woolworths building in New York, constructed in 1913, was a significant landmark, being the world's tallest building for the next 27 years. It had 57 floors and the Otis high-speed electric elevators could reach the top floor in a little over one minute.

I Each elevator used several cables and pulley wheels, though one cable was enough to support the weight of the car. As a further safety feature, an oil-filled shock piston was mounted at the base of the lift shaft to act as a buffer, slowing the car down at a safe rate in the unlikely event of every cable failing as well as the safety brake.

Questions 348 to 352

Do the following statements agree with the information given in the text?

Write:

TRUE if the statement agrees with the information

FALSE if the statement contradicts the information

NOT GIVEN if there is no information on this.

348 Only people could be hoisted with a windlass.

349 Tall commercial buildings were not economic without an elevator.

350 Otis' pattern documents contained a diagram.

351 The first passenger elevator was installed in a hotel.

352 Electric elevators use similar principles to ancient water-wells.

Questions 353 to 356

Answer the questions below.

Choose **ONE NUMBER ONLY** from the text for each answer.

353 In what year did Otis demonstrate his safety brake?

354 In what year did the Grosvenor Hotel open in London?

355 In what year did Otis develop an electric elevator for skyscrapers?

356 In what year was the Woolworths skyscraper no longer the world's tallest building?

Questions 357 to 360

The text has nine paragraphs, **A to I**.

Which paragraph contains the following information?

357 a method that halts the platform when the rope is cut.

358 two methods that take the strain out of lifting.

359 a method that prevents injury if all other safety features fail.

360 a method that applies pressure to a cable to pull it.

General Training Writing

Test A

Writing task 1

You should spend about 20 minutes on this task.

An English-speaking friend has written to you to ask you how your IELTS studies are going.

Write a letter telling your friend how you are preparing for the test.

In your letter:

- say what progress you are making
- explain how you are preparing for the test
- say which section you are finding the most difficult.

Write at least 150 words.

You do NOT need to write any address. Begin your e-mail as follows:

Dear . . . .

Writing task 2

You should spend about 40 minutes on this task.

Opinions vary on whether students should take a gap year before going into higher education.

Discuss the possible advantages and disadvantages of taking a year out.

Do you believe that taking a gap year is a good idea?

Give reasons for your answer and include any relevant experience or knowledge.

Write at least 250 words.

General Training Reading

Test B

Section 1

Questions 361 to 374

Read the text and answer Questions 361 to 367.

USE THE RIGHT TYPE OF FIRE EXTINGUISHER!

Fire extinguishers come in different types depending on the material combusted.

The five main types of fire extinguisher are described below.

Pressurized water

Used for Class A fires only.

Carbon-dioxide

Used for Class E fires because it does not damage electrical equipment such as computers.

Limited use for Class B fires because there is a risk of re-ignition due to a lack of cooling.

Foam-filled

Used for Class B fires. Also used for Class A fires, though not in confined spaces. They are NOT for electrical equipment fires or cooking oil.

Dry powder

Used for Class A, B, C and E fires, with specialist powders for Class D fires.

Smothers the fire but does not cool it or penetrate very well so there is a risk of re-ignition.

Wet chemical

Used for Class F fires, especially high temperature deep fat fryers.

There are six classifications of combustible material as shown below.

Class A: flammable organic solids (eg wood, paper, coal, plastics, textiles)

Class B: flammable liquids (eg gasoline, spirits) but not cooking oil

Class C: flammable gas (eg propane, butane)

Class D: combustible metals (eg magnesium, lithium)

Class E: electrical equipment (eg computers, photocopiers)

Class F: cooking oil and fat

The above classifications apply to Europe and Australia.

Questions 361 to 367

Do the following statements agree with the information given in the text?

Write:

TRUE if the statement agrees with the information

FALSE if the statement contradicts the information

NOT GIVEN if there is no information on this.

361 Class A fires can be tackled with three types of extinguisher.

362 A gasoline fire extinguished with carbon-dioxide might ignite again.

363 Flammable liquids are more likely to reignite than flammable solids.

364 Foam-filled extinguishers can be used on fires involving plastics.

365 Foam-filled extinguishers should NOT be used outdoors.

366 Cooking oil fires should only be tackled with Class F fire extinguishers.

367 Only one type of fire extinguisher is suitable for a lithium battery fire.

Read the text below and answer Questions 368 to 374.

CONTRACT OF EMPLOYMENT

A Macleods is a soft fruit farm, situated approximately 20 km east of Dundee near the village of Muirdrum. The farm is off the Arbroath Road and clearly signposted. Please see the website for a map and travel details.

B You must bring all essential paperwork, including your letter of acceptance, your passport, National ID card, and a work permit if you are not an EU citizen. If you are a student please bring proof of this. Two passport photographs are required.

C You can stay in our modern and clean caravans. They have two bedrooms, each with a single bed, a fully equipped kitchen, a shower and toilet. There is a fee of £4 per day, which includes gas, electric and laundry use. A breakages deposit of £50 is required which will be returned to you in full when you leave, provided that nothing has been damaged.

D The farm consists of 40 hectares of strawberries and 2 hectares of other soft fruits under the cover of polythene tunnels. We use the table-top system so all the fruit is picked at waist level rather than on the ground.

E This means that you are paid harvest-worker piece rates. You will earn a fixed amount per kilogram of fruit picked, so the more you pick, the more you earn. A good picker can earn upwards of £300 per week. You will receive your wages in cash at the end of the week together with a payslip.

F Our polythene tunnels provide protection from the weather but we can still have problems linked to insects, plant diseases or changes in customer demand, meaning that we cannot promise you any work.

G We reserve the legal right to dismiss any employee who is guilty of serious misconduct or who fails to adhere to our health and safety procedures.

Questions 368 to 374

The text has seven sections, **A to G**.

Choose the correct heading for the sections **A**, **B**, **C**, **D**, **E**, **F** and **G** from the list of headings below.

List of headings

i.	Accommodation and charges
ii.	No guarantee of employment
iii.	Bad weather
iv.	Sheltered picking
v.	Documents
vi.	Contract terminated
vii.	Hours of work
viii.	Location
ix.	Piece work
x.	Travel information

368 Section A

369 Section B

370 Section C

371 Section D

372 Section E

373 Section F

374 Section G

Section 2

Questions 375 to 387

Read the text below and answer Questions 375 to 380.

How to create a blog

A blog is an online journal of your ideas, thoughts or opinions on a topic that interests you. Topics tend to be news orientated to reflect current issues or events. Blogs are often linked to web pages to give a website an up-to-date feel, but you can also create stand-alone blogs. A blogging service will provide you with a free account and a selection of templates that enable you to customize the layout and colours of your blog. Blogs are easier to create than web pages and are more interactive. It is possible to add pictures to your blog and links to other websites that visitors might find useful.

Sharing information

Before you post a blog you need to decide whether it is to be made public or kept private. Public information can be seen be any internet user. Private information is restricted to people you choose; for example, friends and family. You can also password protect your blog so that it can be accessed only by users who have logged in. Guest users are sometimes permitted to see some but not all of the blog articles.

How to post information

Readers are invited to respond to your blog by clicking on a 'leave a comment' link. Typically, a series of dialogue boxes appear, inviting the reader to enter the following pieces of information:

- the blogger's real name or a blogging name
- an e-mail address
- a website address if they have one
- a title for the article
- the text that the blogger wishes to post, which is the main part of the blog, usually written in a conversational tone.

The replies to your blog are date and time stamped with the most recent blog displayed first. You will need to update your blog frequently and to respond to blogger's comments promptly if you wish to maintain the interest of your visitors. If other bloggers' comments are not to your liking you can choose to delete them.

Questions 375 to 380

Complete the flow chart below.

Choose **NO MORE THAN TWO WORDS** from the text for each answer.

Creating a blog

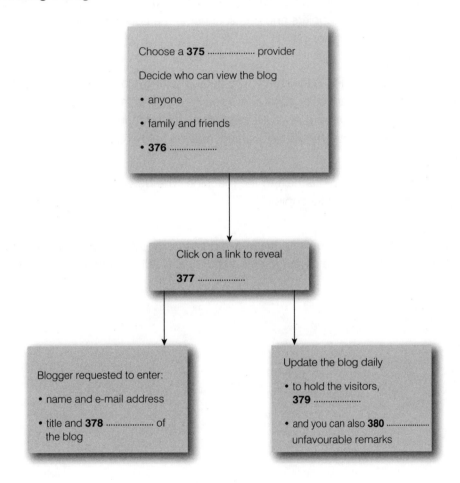

Choose a **375** .... provider

Decide who can view the blog

• anyone

• family and friends

• **376** ....

Click on a link to reveal

377 ....

Blogger requested to enter:

• name and e-mail address

• title and **378** .... of the blog

Update the blog daily

• to hold the visitors, **379** ....

• and you can also **380** .... unfavourable remarks

Read the text below and answer Questions 381 to 387.

Print, copy and scan

The library has print, copy and scan provision. A universal swipe card is available from the card vending machine near the check-out desk. The card costs $2 and will show a balance of $1 when swiped through a machine for the first time. There are two laser printers, two photocopiers and one scanner in the Lower library and one laser printer and one photocopier in the Upper library.

Laser printing
You can print from any PC in the library. The default setting is black and white double-sided printing. If you want color prints or single-sided copies then click on 'Properties' to see the drop down menu. Any URL addresses in a document will automatically print in blue. Please note that your document may be held in a queue.

Photocopying
Please follow the instructions next to the machine. The default setting is Letter size single-sided black and white copies.

Scanning
You can scan your documents to an e-mail address or a USB stick. Please note that any color in a document is detected automatically and will be charged accordingly.

TABLE 5.1

	PRINT/COPY/SCAN CHARGES		
	LASER PRINTING	**PHOTOCOPYING**	
		Single-sided	**Double-sided**
Black and white Letter size	10 cents per side	14 cents	21 cents
Black and white Ledger size	–	24 cents	36 cents
Color Letter size	50 cents per side	70 cents	$1.05
Color Ledger size	–	$1.20	$1.80

SCANNING: 2 cents in black and white, and 4 cents in colour.

Questions 381 to 387

Classify the following statements as referring to:

    A Printer

    B Copier

    C Scanner

    D All three machines.

381 It does not take Ledger size paper.

382 It is not found in the Upper library.

383 Takes a swipe card.

384 You may have to wait for your document to appear.

385 It is the most expensive per side.

386 It cannot automatically print in color.

387 It costs twice as much in color as in black and white.

Section 3

Questions 388 to 400

Read the passage and answer questions 388 to 400.

Old dogs and new tricks

The first days of an animal's life play a major part in shaping its future.

Cormorant birds are used in China and Japan to catch fish in a traditional method of river fishing that dates back thousands of years. A cormorant dives under the water, catches a fish, and then clings to a bamboo pole that the fisherman swings into the boat. It is easy to train a cormorant to behave like this because the bird has been imprinted on the fisherman instead of its natural mother. The fisherman imprints the cormorant on himself by appearing to the chick when it hatches out of the egg. The young bird mistakes the fisherman for the mother bird and bonds with him, responding to his voice and, later, swimming alongside his boat. This 'follow response' is nature's way of preventing young birds from straying from their mother. The process of imprinting lasts for a period of up to two days after hatching. After this sensitive period the effect of the imprinting remains unchanged for the lifetime of the bird and cannot be reversed.

Dogs, cats, sheep, horses and other animals go through a process of imprinting similar to birds. In the case of dogs, the sensitive period lasts for up to 12 weeks. During this time the puppy can imprint on both its natural mother and on humans. Puppies are born blind and deaf, and naturally stay close to their mothers so they do not need an immediate 'follow response'. The sensitive period lasts from the second week to the fourteenth week of life. It is critical that a dog is socialized with other dogs, family pets and with people within this time frame. If the basic social behaviour is not imprinted in a puppy by the fourteenth week it will lead to behavioural problems later in life that are difficult to change.

A puppy should be left with its natural mother and the litter for several weeks before being socialized with people. If a puppy is taken away from its natural mother too early and handled by people then it sees humans as its natural companions and dogs as complete strangers. Dogs that have only been socialized with people are likely to be aggressive towards another person's dog or even attack it. Conversely, a dog that has been kept with the mother and litter for too long will not regard humans as companions and is more likely to be aggressive towards people and bite them. Dogs that have not been adequately socialized with both dogs and people can be difficult to control and will not respond to training.

Negative experiences with humans during the imprinting stage can have lasting effects on a dog. It is a cliché, but bad behaviour in a dog is usually the fault of its owner. A rescue dog that was neglected and abused by its owner is likely to remain nervous and fearful of humans. It is possible for a dog to overcome behavioural problems that originate from imprinting but it requires a lot of training and may not be completely successful. Negative behaviours are often reinforced inadvertently when a dog receives more attention for behaving badly than for behaving well.

In obedience training, the dog is taught to respond to basic commands such as sit, stay, down and release. In one training technique, the owner shouts a command – for example, sit – and if the dog acts accordingly it is rewarded with its favourite toy and is verbally praised. The dog associates the action of sitting with praise from its owner and learns to comply. Punishment and negative experiences are best avoided to ensure a confident, happy and obedient dog. Even an old dog can be taught new tricks, or at least new behaviours, with training every day.

Not all dog behaviour can be explained by imprinting and training. Generations of breeding in captivity has domesticated dogs so that they can live in people's homes as pets, or as working animals. Dogs have been selectively bred to have their natural abilities enhanced or suppressed to suit the needs of man. For example, Border Collies and Belgian Shepherd dogs are pure-bred to herd sheep and protect them, more so when a dog has been imprinted on the flock. Spaniels and Retrievers are used as gun dogs to retrieve game birds for hunters. Scent hounds like the Beagle and the Fox Hound are used for their extra keen sense of smell when sniffing and tracking prey like rabbits and foxes. Some dogs, like Pit Bull Terriers, have been deliberately bred for fighting and can make dangerous pets. It is worth remembering that all dogs have been domesticated from wolves, so any dog has the potential to 'bite the hand that feeds it', no matter how well it has been socialized and trained.

Questions 388 to 392

Do the following statements agree with the information given in the text?

Write:

TRUE if the statement agrees with the information

FALSE if the statement contradicts the information

NOT GIVEN if there is no information on this.

388 Cormorants imprinted on fishermen are difficult to train.

389 Imprinting stops young birds from getting separated from their mother.

390 Chicks are sensitive to imprinting for up to 48 hours after hatching.

391 Imprinting in birds is temporary.

392 Puppies can only imprint on other dogs and humans.

Questions 393 to 396

Choose the correct letter **A**, **B**, **C** or **D** for the question based on the General Reading Passage.

393 Socialization of puppies is very important

    A because they cannot hear or see anything.
    B for developing an immediate follow response.
    C for the first twelve weeks of their life.
    D between the second and fourteenth weeks.

394 Imprinting in puppies

    A is complete by the fourteenth week.
    B lasts for twelve weeks from birth.
    C is impossible to change.
    D occurs only with the natural mother.

395 A puppy that is handled and petted too soon will not

    A be happy with people.

    B be happy with dogs.

    C be happy with dogs and people.

    D have behavioural problems.

396 Bad behaviour is often

    A a cliché.

    B the fault of the dog rather than the owner.

    C encouraged by mistake.

    D due to insufficient training.

Questions 397 to 400

Choose **FOUR** letters **A** to **I**.

The writer describes how a dog can be trained and how its behaviour is instinctive.

Which **FOUR** of the following methods encourage good behaviour in dogs?

    A receiving punishment for bad behaviour

    B daily training

    C by being made to comply

    D using words of approval

    E by choosing a suitable breed

    F by acknowledging bad behaviour

    G by teaching new tricks

    H by using the toy it likes most

    I by encouraging the wolf instincts.

397

398

399

  400

General Training Writing

Test B

Writing task 1

You should spend about 20 minutes on this task.

You have recently bought a DVD player from an online shop. The web page said that it would play MP3 discs but after taking it home you find out that it will only play CDs and DVDs.

Write an e-mail letter to the store manager. In your e-mail:

- **say who you are;**
- **explain the problem;**
- **say what action you would like the store to take.**

Write at least 150 words.

You do NOT need to write any address. Begin your e-mail as follows:

Dear Sir/Madam

Writing task 2

You should spend about 40 minutes on this task.

Some people believe that schoolchildren should be made to wear a uniform. Others feel that children should be free to choose their own clothes.

Discuss both sides of the argument.

Do you agree or disagree with pupils wearing uniforms?

Give reasons for your answer and include any relevant examples from your own knowledge or experiences.

Write at least 250 words.

Audio-Scripts for the Listening Tests

Test 1

Section 1

MAN: Good morning. Student Services.

STUDENT: Hello. Is that the accommodation office?

MAN: Yes it is. How can I help you?

STUDENT: I'm trying to find a place to live. Can you help me please?

MAN: Are you with the English Language School?

STUDENT: Yes I have enrolled on a course that starts in four weeks.

MAN: Well we can offer you three types of accommodation. Do you know what you're looking for?

STUDENT: No I don't. Can you tell me what the different types are please?

MAN: Yes certainly. The main types of accommodation are Halls of Residence, student flats or homestay.

STUDENT: Oh, I see. Can you tell me about the Halls please?

MAN:	Let me see. The Halls of Residence are about 20 minutes' walk from the campus. They cost £60 per week. It's self- **[Q1]** catering only and there is a minimum stay of <u>40 weeks</u>.
STUDENT:	My course lasts eight weeks so this is more than I need. What else did you say you have?
MAN:	Well, there are student flats owned by private landlords. These can be a few miles from the University. They charge a minimum of £75 per week **[Q2]** and you may need a <u>deposit</u> as well as a reference.
STUDENT:	This might be difficult for me. What about homestay? I've heard of it but can you tell me more about it, please?
MAN:	These are family homes and cost from £100 to £150 per **[Q3]** week with a minimum stay of <u>four weeks</u>.
STUDENT:	Yes. This seems like a good idea. Can you tell me more, please?
MAN:	**[Q4]** You have your own room and the fee covers <u>breakfast</u> and **[Q5]** <u>dinner</u> during weekdays, with lunch included at the weekends. I can send you more details through the post or by e-mail.
STUDENT:	I'm living with a friend at the moment. Can you post it to me at her address?
MAN:	Yes, that's possible. I can do it for you today.
STUDENT:	That's fine. Thank you.

- -

MAN:	Before I send you the information I need your address details and some personal information. Can I have your family name, please?
STUDENT:	Yes its Li.
MAN:	Is that L double E.
<u>STUDENT</u>:	**[Q6]** No. It's L I.
MAN:	And your first name?
STUDENT:	It's Mike, spelt M I K E.
MAN:	What nationality are you?
STUDENT:	I'm a British-born Chinese.
MAN:	OK. Can I have your current address, please?
STUDENT:	Yes, it's 108 Archer Park, Middleton, Manchester.

MAN: And the postcode please.

STUDENT: **[Q7]** It's M24 7AB.

MAN: And your telephone number.

STUDENT: **[Q8]** Yes, it's 0161 343651.

MAN: Now there are eight possible homestay providers near the English Language School but they might not all be suitable. I need to check your preferences. Do you smoke?

STUDENT: No, I don't, so I'd like a non-smoking home please.

MAN: Do you have a special diet? Are you vegetarian for example?

STUDENT: **[Q9]** I eat meat but I don't eat fish.

MAN: And do you have any medical conditions?

STUDENT: No, I have no health problems.

MAN: What about family pets. Do you like cats and dogs?

STUDENT: Well I like cats but not dogs.

MAN: OK. There's just one more thing. Do you want a room with your own private bathroom? This might cost a little bit extra.

STUDENT: I would prefer it as long as it's not too much more.

MAN: **[Q10]** Well, we have a couple of providers that are suitable for you. I'll post the information out today. Please contact this office as soon as you have made your decision. Otherwise you might find that your room has been taken.

STUDENT: OK I'll do that. Thank you. Bye.

Section 2

Good morning everyone, and thank you for attending today's Open Day at the International Student's Centre, or **ISC building**. I'm John; one of the College's resident students. We'll be making a brief tour of the campus first. Please feel free to ask questions as we walk along, and I'll do my best to answer them.

[Q11] Now, from where we are standing you can see the **Arts centre**. It's the circular building directly opposite. The Centre is open to both students and the public. There are weekly classes in drawing and painting, music and drama; also photography and ceramics. Directly behind the Arts Centre is

[Q12] **the Sports hall** which houses a fitness room, badminton courts, showers and a steam-room. Once again, these facilities are open to the public, though a charge is made if you don't have a sports card. Next to the Arts Centre, a little way up the road, is the **Reed dining room** with its adjoining café.

[Q13] The Reed dining room is named after Dr John Reed, that's **R double E, D** the last Principal of the College…. OK, let's take a stroll along Campus Road. This is a pedestrians only road so there's no need to worry about cars. I'll say a bit more about cars

[Q14] later. The first building, here on your left, is the **Information Services** building, which houses the Main Library, IT services and also a Media room. Notice the covered walkway to keep you dry when walking between the Information Services and ISC buildings…. Right, let's continue along Campus Road a little bit more. Just coming up on the right is the

[Q15] Students' Union building and bar, and behind it, though you can't see it from here, is the **Union Shop**. Here you can buy stationery items, second-hand books and University merchandise. The Union Shop will also buy second-hand books from students.

– –

Any questions so far? … No? Right in that case, let's carry on…. Now, please keep out of the cycle lane as we walk around the corner. OK, we can stop

[Q16] here for a minute. The **car park**, on the left, houses a covered bicycle park. You can use the car park and the bicycle racks but you do need a permit. These are available from the Hospitality Services Office which can be found in the Students' Union building. There are a limited number of spaces, and permits are issued on a first-come first-served basis. The access to the car park is from Campus Road on foot, but <u>the entrance for cars is from</u>

[Q17] **North Road**. For students arriving by bus, the nearest bus stop is in North Road, just past the start of Campus Road. A bus stops here every 10 minutes between 8 o'clock and half past nine, Monday to Friday. Outside of these hours a bus stops on North Road every 30 minutes between 10 o'clock and 6 pm.

[Q18] Next, I'd just like to draw your attention to the **Education Centre** <u>over to</u> <u>your right</u>, opposite the bike shed. Most of your lectures will be held in the ISC building but some will be delivered in the Education Centre.
Behind the Education Centre there are two Halls of Residence. These are both self-catering. <u>Moore Hall</u> is over to the left, but you can't see it from here. Oh no, sorry that's wrong. It's Hepworth Hall to the left. The Hall was named after Barbara Hepworth, a contemporary of Moore. Hepworth is spelt

[Q19] **H E P W O R T H**. Moore Hall is the building that sticks out on the right. It was named after the famous English artist and sculptor, Sir Henry Moore.

[Q20] <u>Moore is spelt</u> **M double O, R E**.... Well, thank you for your attention this morning. We'll now return to the ISC building for refreshments, when I'll be happy to answer any questions you may have.

Section 3

INTERVIEWER: Good morning. We're pleased to welcome Professor Louis Counter from the European Numeracy Centre who has come here today to talk about Numeracy Week.

Professor Counter, I'd like to start by asking, what is Numeracy Week and who is it aimed at? Is it mostly for young people or adults?

PROFESSOR: Well, Numeracy Week is part of a strategy to improve mathematical **[Q21]** skills throughout the European Union. It aims <u>to raise awareness that improving your numeracy can be a rewarding experience for people of all ages</u>, not just one particular age group.

INTERVIEWER: Oh I see. And why are mathematical skills so important in today's society?

PROFESSOR: A lack of numerical skill prevents people from applying for better paid jobs, or from retraining, or perhaps from entering higher education.

What's more, there is a knock-on effect on future generations when **[Q22]** parents are unable to assist their children with maths homework. <u>A relationship exists between success in the classroom and parental input at home.</u>

INTERVIEWER: So what is the main message you would like to send out to people who have difficulties with numbers?

PROFESSOR: **[Q23]** Well people should not feel embarrassed about their <u>lack of mathematical knowledge. It's a widespread problem, as in fact is literacy.</u> I would like to see more people enrolling on numeracy courses, no matter how poor someone perceives his or her numeracy to be.

INTERVIEWER: And what are the key skills covered in these type of classes?

PROFESSOR: Well in the past, classes tended to focus on basic arithmetic skills **[Q24]** without sufficient real-life context. <u>Today we like to view numeracy from a vocational perspective. That is to say, in relation to the type of work you do.</u> Of course, number skills remain useful in a general way as well; for example, with financial transactions,

	such as paying for goods and checking the change you receive, or working out the savings to be made on sale items, as well as budgeting for things like vacations, so that you don't get into debt.
INTERVIEWER:	Well yes. I can see the benefits of all those things. And can you tell me the main reasons why people attend numeracy classes?
PROFESSOR:	Well each individual will have their own personal reasons, and these can differ widely from person to person.
INTERVIEWER:	**[Q25]** I realize that. Do you think that people are looking to <u>fill in</u> the <u>gaps in their education left by a poor performance at school?</u>
PROFESSOR:	Yes, that can be the case. Some people return to the classroom to prove to themselves that they can be successful academically, whilst others want to pass an exam that they failed previously. The sense of achievement helps to build confidence and self-esteem.
INTERVIEWER:	Well it seems that people have nothing to lose and everything to gain. Thank you Professor.

- -

INTERVIEWER:	Did you catch that question, Professor? One of our listeners would like to know more about the numeracy curriculum.
PROFESSOR:	Well, the elements of numeracy are the same worldwide. As a first **[Q26]** step <u>it's essential to memorize the multiplication tables</u>.
INTERVIEWER:	Hasn't the electronic calculator taken over most of this work, Professor?
PROFESSOR:	It's true that electronic calculators can do many calculations quickly, **[Q27]** but <u>mental arithmetic remains a key skill</u>. You cannot use a calculator to cancel fractions for example.
INTERVIEWER:	No, er… that's true… and what about the metric system, as we're part of Europe?
PROFESSOR:	**[Q28]** Yes, I'm glad you mentioned that. It's vital for people <u>to get to grips with the metric system of measurement</u>, which must be included in any curriculum.

INTERVIEWER: And what about the workplace; you mentioned a vocational perspective earlier?

PROFESSOR: That's right. Some employees need to read information from graphs and charts, or from tables. And it's quite common to have to record measurements and take readings at work.

[Q29] <u>Some people struggle to read instrument dials properly</u>. This could create a problem if you wanted a job with the postal service, for example, where you might need to weigh items on a scale or balance.

INTERVIEWER: ... And I guess there are many other jobs and careers where numeracy skills are vital.

PROFESSOR: So much so, that <u>many employers insist on testing numeracy</u> **[Q30]** <u>skills as a means of screening-out unsuitable candidates</u>.

INTERVIEWER: ... I see. Yes, as part of shortlisting. Well thank you once again, Professor. There's plenty for our listeners to think about.

Section 4

Hi! I'm Dr Scott Stormwell and I'm going to talk briefly about hurricanes and tornadoes. I'll be covering how and where they form, then I'll move on to describe the hurricane naming system; by that I mean the use of male and female first names like Hurricane Calvin or Hurricane Julia.

And whilst we're on the subject of names I'll also be explaining the differences between names like cyclone, hurricane, typhoon, tornado and twister. Some of these names are used interchangeably to refer to the same phenomena, which **[Q31]** can lead to confusion, but I'll be keeping to the strict meteorological definitions.

OK, a twister is the informal name for a tornado; so that's easy. A tornado is a relatively small column of violently rotating air formed over land during a severe thunderstorm. The majority of tornadoes are less than 200 metres in diameter, and they spin with high wind speeds, typically up to 200 miles per hour; that's **[Q32]** 300 kilometres per hour, which makes them very destructive. The tornado, or twister, forms inside thick storm clouds when warm air, rising from the ground, is forced to spin as it hits cold, fast-moving air from above. If the tornado forms over water, for example a lake or the sea, it becomes a waterspout.

Tornadoes can form in any part of the world but they occur most frequently over flat areas in America; typically in the central and southern states, **[Q33]** reducing in number towards the eastern seaboard. The western half of America is rarely affected. So the worst-affected states tend to be Kansas, Missouri, Iowa and Kentucky, down to Texas, Mississippi and Louisiana, but not exclusively these places.

Right, let's move on to cyclones. These are massive; several hundred miles in **[Q34]** diameter, sometimes over 1,000 kilometres. Cyclones form over warm seas, typically above 25 degrees C. As the warm, moist air from the ocean evaporates, it rises to create an area of low pressure beneath. This depression drags in the **[Q35]** surrounding air which then swirls in the same direction as the earth rotates. Speeds are usually lower than those in a tornado but they can still build to 150 miles per hour or 240 kilometres, sufficient to wreak tremendous damage when the cyclone reaches land, where it eventually dies out. The centre of the storm contains a calm region, the eye of the cyclone, which can be tens of kilometres wide.

So what about hurricanes and typhoons? Well this is straightforward. Cyclones, hurricanes and typhoons describe the same type of cyclonic storm. However, the word cyclone tends to be used with storms that form below the equator of the earth, whereas hurricanes and typhoons are cyclones that form above the equator. **[Q36]** <u>Typhoon is the favoured term in Asia and Hurricane in America</u>.

Right, I mentioned at the beginning of the talk that I'd be looking into the hurricane naming system, so that's what I'd like to do now…. You've probably all heard names like Hurricane Katrina and Hurricane Andrew because these hurricanes were two of America's largest natural disasters. But how did the naming system originate and how were the names chosen? Before I go into this I need to make a distinction between a tropical storm and a tropical cyclone, or hurricane. <u>A tropical storm is referred to as a hurricane</u> when the storm achieves a sustained <u>wind speed in excess of</u> 40 miles per hour, that's
[Q37] <u>65 kilometres per hour</u>. It's the tropical storm that's given a name first. So, for example, tropical storm William becomes Hurricane William if its speed exceeds 40 miles per hour. There's no Hurricane William if the tropical storm dissipates before it reaches 40 miles per hour.

Now, in the early days of weather forecasting, by that I mean <u>pre-1940</u>, hurricanes **[Q38]** weren't usually named; <u>forecasts simply referred to the storm in terms of its position</u>, ie latitude and longitude. However, this became problematic as a means of tracking individual hurricanes so the most severe hurricanes were given names, though not in any systematic way. Initially, names were chosen at random, or they might reflect the name of a place in the vicinity of the storm. The current official naming system originated in America in 1945, and was first applied to storms within the Western Pacific Ocean. Only female names were chosen <u>until 1979</u>, similar to the **[Q39]** naming of boats and ships, <u>after which time male and female names were alternated</u>.

Today, there are official lists of names for most of the world's oceans, in most cases at least 20 names per ocean, per year, are made available. The names are placed in alphabetical order, so the first tropical storm of the season will start with the letter A, and the next storm will have a name starting with the letter B, and so on. **[Q40]** Complete sets of names are drawn up to cover <u>several years</u> of storms, after which time the <u>names can be recycled</u>.

One final thing; the names Hurricane Katrina and Hurricane Andrew will never appear again; the name of any destructive hurricane is always retired from the lists of names.

Test 2

Section 1

FEMALE GUIDE:	Hello. Walking Tours.
STUDENT:	Hi. Is that Oxford guided walks?
FEMALE GUIDE:	Yes, it is. Would you like to book a tour around Oxford?
STUDENT:	Well, I have already booked a tour but I need to cancel it. Two of my friends can no longer make it on Friday so we have decided not to go ahead. I'd like a refund if possible.
FEMALE GUIDE:	Oh I see. And which tour had you booked for please?
STUDENT:	**[Q81]** It was the <u>Harry Potter Tour</u>.
FEMALE GUIDE:	OK. Do you have the booking reference number? It's on the ticket.
STUDENT:	I haven't got it with me.
FEMALE GUIDE:	Well, when did you book the tour for? Do you remember?
STUDENT:	**[Q82]** It was for Friday the <u>15th of June</u> at 2 o'clock.
FEMALE GUIDE:	OK. Let me check your name so I can find you on the system. You are?
STUDENT:	It's Dave Chew.
FEMALE GUIDE:	That's C H double O is it?
STUDENT:	**[Q83]** It's <u>C H E W</u>.
FEMALE GUIDE:	Right, I'll just get the details on the screen….
STUDENT:	I live in Plumstead, London.
FEMALE GUIDE:	And did you pay by credit card or debit card?
STUDENT:	**[Q84]** I paid by debit card for <u>myself and four other people</u>.
FEMALE GUIDE:	Now there is a cancellation fee of 20% of the entire booking.
STUDENT:	I didn't know there was a cancellation fee.
FEMALE GUIDE:	**[Q85]** Yes, I'm afraid so. You <u>paid £50</u>, so the fee works out at £10. That means I can refund £40 back to your card. Do you want me to go ahead with this?
STUDENT:	If I change to another day will you still charge the fee?
FEMALE GUIDE:	If you wish to postpone you can do so for a flat fee of £5.

STUDENT:	Well that sounds better. I'll get back to you with the new booking details once I've spoken to my friends.

FEMALE GUIDE:	So what date would you like to book the new tour?
STUDENT:	Well, Friday week would be ideal.
FEMALE GUIDE:	And is this for the Harry Potter Tour again?
STUDENT:	We'd like to try a different tour. The Inspector Morse Tour, please.
FEMALE GUIDE:	Ah. Now we only run that tour on a Saturday. Will that be all right for you?
STUDENT:	Yes, that's better actually. Oh, and how long does the tour last please?
FEMALE GUIDE:	It's about a couple of hours like the other tours. We depart at a quarter to two sharp and I recommend that you aim to arrive by half past one.
STUDENT:	Right, that's fine. I can go ahead and book.
FEMALE GUIDE:	So that's five adults for the Inspector Morse Tour starting **[Q86]** at a quarter to two on Saturday the 23rd of June. Is that right?
STUDENT:	It's only four adults now.
FEMALE GUIDE:	Ah, I see. I'll need to recalculate it. The Morse Tour is £13 each, whereas the Potter Tour was £10. So it works out at £52, plus £5 for the change of date, making a total of £57. And you have **[Q87]** already paid £50, so I will need to charge you an extra £7. Is that OK for you?
STUDENT:	That's great.
FEMALE GUIDE:	And what is your debit card number again, please? That's the 16 digit number on the front of your card.
STUDENT:	**[Q88]** Yes, I have it. It's 5471 4710 2382 3900.
FEMALE GUIDE:	Now if you have a pen and paper handy I'll give you the new booking reference number.
STUDENT:	OK, I'm ready.
FEMALE GUIDE:	**[Q89]** Right, it's M236YC, and I'll post out your new tickets today.
STUDENT:	And tell me again, where do we set out from?

FEMALE GUIDE: We meet up in Broad Street, in the centre of Oxford, in the pedestrianized zone adjacent to Balliol College.

STUDENT: Is that near to Oxford Railway Station?

FEMALE GUIDE: It's about 1 kilometre from the station. No more than 15 minutes' walk.

STUDENT: Will you be our guide?

FEMALE GUIDE: **[Q90]** Yes. I'm Jane and I'll be your guide for the afternoon. I'll be wearing a wide-brimmed hat with a red bow so you can recognize me.

STUDENT: Oh, that's helpful. See you on Saturday afternoon.

FEMALE GUIDE: Look forward to meeting you. Bye for now.

Section 2

Good morning. Can I have your attention please? I'd like to run through the pro-gramme of events for the Northern Ireland field trip. I'll explain the travel arrange-ments in more detail shortly. Can I point out that the trip is not compulsory so you may opt out if you wish. However, we recommend that you go on the field trip because it will increase your knowledge of the

[Q91]   subject. Last year, over <u>seventy-five per cent</u> of students on the trip achieved a top grade in their assignments.

OK, I'll explain the travel arrangements and the costs once again. You'll receive detailed handouts later today, but make your own notes if you wish to. We leave here on Saturday the 10th of September and arrive back the following Saturday, on the 16th. The fee for the field trip is £349; this covers

[Q92]   the cost of the entire eight days, including <u>6 nights'</u> half-board <u>accommoda-tion</u>. You will be responsible for paying for your own lunchtime meals. Your seat on the minibus and the ferry is covered by the deposit of £50, so this leaves an outstanding balance of £299, to be paid by the end of the month. We'll be travelling on the Holyhead to Dublin Ferry which departs Holyhead at twenty to three in the morning. Yes! It really is that late, or

[Q93]   should I say early; and it arrives in Dublin port at about <u>six in the morning</u>, so you'll have to grab some sleep on the minibus and on the ferry. The trip by road from here to the ferry terminal will take at least two hours, and we need to arrive 30 minutes before the ferry sets sail. So I'd like to leave well before midnight. Please be here no later than half-past eleven. Is that

[Q94]   clear? We'll make a brief stop midway <u>for refreshments and to use the toilets</u>.

We can't plan for the weather. However, we will know in advance if the ferry has been cancelled due to adverse weather conditions. If the sea gets too rough we might experience a delay or have to transfer to a later sailing. I suggest that people who experience motion sickness see their pharmacist and medicate themselves accordingly before boarding the ferry. Please note that passengers cannot return to their vehicles to retrieve <u>items</u> once the

[Q95]   ferry sets sail so take <u>essential personal belongings with you</u>.

We won't be stopping in Dublin, so no tour of the Guinness brewery on this trip. Instead we'll be heading for our accommodation in the village of

[Q96]   Dundrum, which is famous for its <u>Norman castle</u>. The journey will take about two hours so we'll stop for a short break en route.

Right. Has everyone received their handouts? The sheet you want has the schedule for each day on the front page and a map on the reverse side. You'll notice that there are six days of activities listed. The morning of Day 1, that's Saturday, is spent travelling to our accommodation. <u>After lunch,</u>

[Q97]   we'll take a <u>walk</u> in the National Trust's nature reserve, <u>by the sea</u>. On the following day, Day 2, if the weather is fine, we can spend all day in the mountains of Mourne; these are made of granite rock. Alternatively, if the weather is poor, we can split the day between a visit to the Silent Valley reservoir, Belfast's water supply, and a visit to the town of Newcastle

[Q98]   followed by a <u>walk in</u> Tollymore <u>Park</u>. These places are shown on your map. On the morning of Day 3 we'll be travelling north to Portrush to our new lodgings. In the afternoon we'll visit the Giant's Causeway. This is Ireland's first world heritage site and a popular tourist destination. People come to see the basalt hexagonal columns created from an outpouring of volcanic magma. Following this, there's a nine-mile walk around the headland to the famous

[Q99]   Carrick-a-rede <u>rope bridge</u>. It's not for the faint hearted, but you don't have to <u>cross</u> it.

Day 4 is a recovery day, with a tour of the Whitewater brewery and a beer-tasting session in the afternoon. On Day 5 we'll visit Londonderry before heading towards the Glenelly valley to see the metamorphic rocks. On our last day we'll travel to Ballycastle with its 150 metre high dolerite

[Q100]   <u>cliffs</u>, which are popular with <u>rock climbers</u>. That's on Day 6. After leaving the cliffs we'll make our way back to Dublin to catch the late ferry home.

Section 3

PAUL: How's the poster presentation going Hannah?

HANNAH: Well I've made a start, but can you help me with the PowerPoint please?

PAUL: Yeah… OK…. Have you created a new folder yet; that's the first thing to do?

HANNAH: I've done it already, but what's the next step?

PAUL: Well what size would you like the poster to be?

HANNAH: I tried putting these four sheets together to make one big sheet but it's still too small.

PAUL: OK, well the paper size is automatically set to 36 high by **[Q101]** 48 wide, <u>but the maximum width is 60</u>. You can select it under page set-up.

HANNAH: No, 48's fine. That's plenty big enough.

PAUL: **[Q102]** Have you decided on a <u>title</u> yet?

HANNAH: Yes it's 'No footprints'.

PAUL: Right, well <u>type it into the box at the top</u>…. Now you need a large font size for the title. <u>A minimum of 96 point</u>, and the main text should not be **[Q103]** less than 26 point… <u>maybe 48 for secondary headings</u>.

HANNAH: Can I change the colour of the background?

PAUL: You can, but don't overdo it. White is fine.

HANNAH: <u>How do I insert my text</u>?

PAUL: **[Q104]** It's easy. <u>Just cut and paste it from your essay</u>.

HANNAH: And can I insert images in the same way?

PAUL: Have these been scanned in or were they taken with a digital camera?

HANNAH: They're mostly photos that I've taken and copied into My Pictures.

PAUL: Let's see. If I click on this picture of a wind turbine… then paste it in… and resize it. OK?

HANNAH: Yes. Will it look all right or do you think it's a bit small?

PAUL: No, it's fine. Just make sure your images are <u>no smaller</u> **[Q105]** <u>than 50 K in size</u>, otherwise they'll look grainy on the poster… you know… er… pixelated. JPEGs look best.

HANNAH: That's great, Paul. I'll carry on now thanks.

PAUL: I'll pop back in a while to see how you're getting on.

PAUL: I see the poster's taking shape now Hannah.

HANNAH: Oh, Hi Paul. I've got all the text in now, and done some editing. What do you think of it so far?

PAUL: I like the piece in the middle box, about offsetting emissions. Where did you get that from?

HANNAH: **[Q106]** Off a web page.

PAUL: OK, fine, but you'll still have to cite it in your references.

HANNAH: Where should I do that?

PAUL: At the end, in the final box on the template.

HANNAH: Do you like the picture of the carbon-cycle?
[Q107] It's from an old school book.

PAUL: Yes, I like the colours; it stands out very well. But I think you should move **[Q108]** it and attach it to the Introduction.

HANNAH: OK, that's a good idea. I'll move it straight away. Now I need to insert this table showing carbon-emissions for different types of personal transport, based on official government figures.

PAUL: Well just hold on a moment. Have you saved your work yet?

HANNAH: No. I'd better do that first. I don't want to lose anything.

PAUL: Right. Now use the paste special command so it imports the table as a graphic file. This is going into the second box is it?

HANNAH: **[Q109]** No, the next one after it.

PAUL: Yes, that looks very neat, but can I make a suggestion?

HANNAH: Yes, go on. What is it?

PAUL: Well, you haven't put your name anywhere. You can put it below the title, though in a smaller font obviously.

HANNAH: OK, I'll do that.

PAUL: And it would look more professional if you inserted the College logo.

HANNAH: Well where can I find it?

PAUL: **[Q110]** Try the College's home page. Put it in the two top corners.
Then you're just about done.

Section 4

Good morning. I'm Professor Menzies, and I've been asked here today to talk about diagrams. By way of introduction, I'd like to run through the history of diagrams from the earliest times... mainly because we need to be clear about what we mean by the word diagram, as opposed to other similar terms such as picture, illustration, or sign.

Historically, it's important to make these distinctions because, for example, rock art can be traced back tens of thousands of years, as in <u>the depiction of wild</u>

[Q111] <u>animals in cave paintings in Europe, or in Aboriginal rock art</u>; these probably reflect early man's respect for animals or have religious significance. Either way, images like this are not classed as diagrams, only pictures or illustrations. Similarly, we can also discount <u>the hieroglyphics</u>, carved into

[Q112] stone in <u>Egyptian writing, where pictures were used to indicate words or sounds</u>. We still use pictures to convey messages today, for example, traffic signs to indicate speed limits, but pictures like this are not classed as diagrams.

Instead, a diagram is a drawing showing a relationship between the objects in the diagram. An early example of a diagram can be found in Pythagoras's theorem of around 500 BC. In this theorem, the square drawn on the longest side of a right-angled triangle has an area equal to the sum of the squares on the other two sides. Three hundred years later, <u>another Greek</u>

[Q113] <u>mathematician, namely Archimedes</u>, also a scientist and astronomer, drew numerous diagrams associated with his many theories, ideas and inventions, which still abound today. For example, Archimedes used geometric drawings to calculate the mathematical constant Pi; the ratio of a circle's circumference to its diameter.

Another well-known type of diagram is the map. Maps can be traced back over 500 years. The Wikipedia dictionary defines a map as a '<u>diagrammatic</u>

[Q114] <u>representation of an area of land or sea</u> showing physical features, cities, roads, etc': for example 'a street map'. The inclusion of axes and co-ordinates in maps and charts had to wait until the 17th century, invented by Descartes. In the modern era we still think of diagrams in terms of maps, charts and

[Q115] graphs, but also as any drawing that <u>aids the comprehension of complex information</u> by displaying it in a visual way. In the mid 19th century, the

[Q116] British nurse <u>Florence Nightingale, used a diagram resembling a pie chart</u> to great effect, when depicting the causes of mortality of injured soldiers.

- -

Mathematics employs a wide range of diagrams particularly in geometry and statistics; examples include graphs, histograms, Venn diagrams, tree diagrams, and box and whisker plots…. So I think it's fair to say that a

[Q117] <u>high proportion of diagrams are linked to mathematical data; but not exclu-</u><u>sively so</u>.
Flow charts are one of the better known non-mathematical diagrams. They were invented in the 1920s and gained popularity in the 1960s with the development of simple computer programs consisting of a set of stored instructions; which is why we're interested in them today. The elements of a flow chart are a series of boxes linked by lines and arrows. The reader starts at the top box and works downwards or sometimes side ways, or even

[Q118] <u>loops back to the original box</u>, depending upon the instructions in the box. Flow charts enable the reader to make the correct decision in response to questions that require either a Yes or a No answer. Typically a

[Q119] flow chart ensures that the <u>correct procedures are followed</u> in business practice, or that the correct sequence of operations are adhered to in a manufacturing process.

All flow charts use a set of geometric shapes. For example: oval-shaped

[Q120] boxes to indicate the start and the end of the flow chart. <u>Rectangles to</u> <u>enclose instructions, stating what action needs to be taken</u>; diamond shapes for decision boxes, where a question has a Yes or No answer. Lines with arrows extend from the decision box to direct the reader to the next piece of information, or process to be carried out.

Test 3

Section 1

CAMPER:	Hello. Is that the Goodnight camping and caravan park?
MANAGER:	Yes it is. How can I help?
CAMPER:	Well I need to know more about your facilities.
MANAGER:	OK. We have over 80 pitches including 20 for caravans. The site has a large kitchen and dining area, toilet and shower facilities, also a **[Q161]** launderette and <u>electricity</u> points.
CAMPER:	A simple grass pitch is fine but can I bring a dog?
MANAGER:	Yes, this is a dog-friendly site. You can bring up to two dogs per pitch, free of charge. What else would you like to know?
CAMPER:	Are campfires and barbecues allowed?
MANAGER:	**[Q162]** Yes they are, but only <u>on the riverbank</u>, away from the tents.
CAMPER:	Well, er, do I need to book in advance or can we just turn up?
MANAGER:	You don't need to make a reservation but we do recommend it for **[Q163]** bank-holiday weekends, and also for <u>large groups</u> of 20 or more.
CAMPER:	Well there are only four of us but I'd like to go ahead and book anyway. Do I book over the phone or online?
MANAGER:	The easiest way is via the website.
CAMPER:	Right. Do you accept credit cards?
MANAGER:	Yes we accept credit cards, debit cards and PayPal. If you prefer not to pay online, you can make a booking by forwarding a cheque for **[Q164]** <u>£20</u>, enclosing details of the dates you want and the number of pitches you need. I'm afraid we cannot refund the deposit if you cancel.
CAMPER:	And what was the tariff again please? I mean per night.
MANAGER:	**[Q165]** Oh yes, sorry I forgot that.... It's <u>£8 per head per night</u>, which includes access to all the facilities.
CAMPER:	OK, well that seems straightforward enough. Now, can you supply firewood?

MANAGER: Yes we do, it's £3 per night, or you can bring your own.

CAMPER: Right, erm, all I need now is your web page address.

- -

MANAGER: Do you have a pen and paper to take down the web page details?

CAMPER: Yes, I'm ready.

MANAGER: Our website is w w w dot goodnightpark dot uk dot com
           [Q166] with <u>goodnightpark</u> written as one word. Have you got it?

CAMPER: Yes thanks.... Oh, I almost forgot. Can you tell me the dates when the
           park is open, please?

MANAGER: Right. We open for the summer season on the 1st of June and close on
           [Q167] the <u>last day of September</u>.

CAMPER: And can we arrive at any time of day?

MANAGER: You need to call in at the reception office between the hours of 8 am
           and 4 pm, but if you have booked online you can turn up as late as
           [Q168] <u>half-past nine in the evening</u>.

CAMPER: Well that's useful to know. We'll be travelling by coach and then by
           bus. We hope to arrive by 3 o'clock in the afternoon but we could
           be delayed by traffic. Looking at the map it's a journey of at least
           [Q169] <u>100 miles</u>.

MANAGER: Where did you say you were travelling from?

CAMPER: It's Chester. Do you know it?

MANAGER: Not very well. But I think you'll use the M5 motorway for most of the
           journey.

CAMPER: OK, there's just one last thing really. Can I have the postcode and the
           GPS co-ordinates of the park if possible, please?

MANAGER: Well I don't have the GPS co-ordinates to hand, but they are on the
           website. The postcode is GL2 7JN. If you put it into a SatNav it will get
           [Q170] you to <u>within 200 metres</u> of the park.

CAMPER: OK, I'll do that. It's a Gloucester postcode isn't it?

MANAGER: Yes, that's right.

CAMPER: Fine, I have all the information I need. I'll book online later today.
           Thanks for your help. Hope to see you in a few weeks. Bye for now.

MANAGER: See you when you arrive. Bye.

Section 2

Hi everyone. It's great to see so many new volunteers here this weekend. We have a wide variety of outdoor work planned, all aimed at improving the countryside and protecting the natural habitat. Don't worry if you haven't done this type of work before, because we'll show you exactly what to do. Also we've got Dave Pritchard with us today, who'll help us to repair the dry stone walls and the paths.

Now I must point out that some of the work is quite difficult and may not be suitable for everyone. So we've decided to split the work into three levels

[Q171] of difficulty, OK; grades 1, 2 and 3. Grade 1 is <u>light work</u>; Grade 2 is moderate work; and Grade 3 is heavy work. I hope that makes sense to everyone. You can always switch groups if you're not happy.

OK, we need some volunteers to help to clear away Himalayan balsam. It's one of several species around here that are not native to this country.

[Q172] <u>It looks like bamboo</u>. This is Grade 1 work so it only needs a low level of fitness. Can I have a show of hands for this job please? Almost anyone

[Q173] can do this work. Let's see that's 1, 2, 3, 4… <u>OK that's 5 people</u> for clearing bamboo. Is there anyone else? No?

Now <u>litter and rubbish</u> are a major problem in this area. Tidying it up will

[Q174] take a <u>moderate amount of effort</u>. The <u>main task is litter picking</u> and if there is enough time, clearing vegetation from the paths. Do I have <u>two volunteers</u> please?… Right, it's that lady there, and the man with the hat. Thank you.

[Q175] Remember, this is Grade 2 work that requires an <u>average level of fitness</u>. Are you OK with that? Right, the rest of the group can help with fencing, walling and the access paths.

[Q176] Now fencing is Grade 2 work, but <u>building walls is heavy, Grade 3 work. You will need to be very fit to do Grade 3 work</u>, and you'll also need to be wearing protective footwear, which means steel-toe boots not just any old shoes. If you don't have the right boots then you'll have to help with the fencing and paths. We have 10 people left, so how many are happy to do the stone-walling?

[Q177] … Right that's 1, 2, 3, 4, 5… <u>I count 6</u>. Please be careful and work at a steady pace. You'll need to save some energy for the tree planting tomorrow. Are there any questions?… No? Then let's split into our groups and make the most of the fine weather. We'll stop at 11 o'clock for a cup of tea and a biscuit.

Hi, I'm Dave and I'll be helping you to repair this stretch of dry-stone wall today. There are six volunteers, so if we can split into three groups of two people that would be helpful. That gives us two people working at each end of the wall, and two people working in the middle. Now, we don't want to see one end of the wall going up quicker than the other; it's important to keep the wall level as it goes up, otherwise we'll end up with a problem in the middle.

[Q178] The largest rocks form the base of the wall, which is helpful because we don't have to lift them too far, but we'll also keep a few of the bigger stones for higher up.

OK. If you look at this damaged section of wall, you can see that it's really

[Q179] two walls with a gap in between. The gap in the centre is filled with the smallest stones. These have a rounded shape and are known as 'hearting' or packing stones. Don't just throw them into the wall. Place these packing stones carefully into the gap because they help to keep the other stones in place.

[Q180] The large, long stones, like this one here, should be placed across the full width of the wall, from one face to the other. For appearance sake, try to keep the stones with the best-looking faces for the outside of the wall. Right, let's clear away some of these fallen stones so we don't trip over them, and then get started.

Section 3

INTERVIEWER: Hello Mike.

MANAGER: Hi Dave. Come in and take a seat.

INTERVIEWER: Thanks. Can you explain to our students how a work-placement increases their chances of securing a job after they've graduated.

MANAGER: Well, the most obvious thing to say here is that many graduates go on to work for the company that offered them the placement experience in the first place.

INTERVIEWER: Yes, I can see why this might happen. But in a more general sense, what are the benefits of a placement?

MANAGER: **[181]** Right; placements give students a real insight into the culture of the workplace, and how they can transfer their knowledge and skills to it. By drawing on placement experiences, graduates are able to sell themselves more effectively when applying for a job and **[182]** compiling a CV. And at the interview stage, graduates appear more confident and can express themselves in the language appropriate to their chosen career.

INTERVIEWER: OK, fine; and what about the employer's perspective on work-placements? How do employers benefit?

MANAGER: Employers can see how a prospective employee performs within a team, also whether they are a good communicator and problem **[183]** solver. It's a job with duties and responsibilities at a level that an undergraduate should cope with. Work-placements help employers to recruit the right person for the job.

INTERVIEWER: And what about when the student returns to college at the end of the placement? What advantages does the work experience bring to college work?

MANAGER: Well the majority of students find their placements to be positive learning experiences. Work experience enables students to make **[184]** links between theory and practice, which should facilitate academic learning.

INTERVIEWER: Right, and just one last thing on placements; what about mentorship and support during the work-placement?

MANAGER: Each student has a mentor in the workplace and a placement **[185]** tutor – <u>an academic member of staff</u> – who makes regular visits to the workplace to discuss the student's progress and, if necessary, <u>resolve any problems or issues</u>.

INTERVIEWER: OK, thanks Mike.

- -

INTERVIEWER: Now continuing with our theme of graduate employment, we're going to talk about soft skills – what they are and why you need them. Mike… Can you define what is meant by soft skills?

MANAGER: Yes. Soft skills are an extension of what I mentioned earlier, when I spoke about team-working and communication. It's not sufficient these days to have only the know-how – by that I mean the technical skills to do the job – employers also look for personal qualities and interpersonal skills.

INTERVIEWER: And why are personal qualities so important in the business world?

MANAGER: Well, employers want people that are going to add value to their business and not detract from it. Simple things like <u>lack of</u> **[186]** <u>punctuality – showing up on time</u> and being dependable will always be important to any company, as are honesty and integrity. These personal characteristics are an inherent part of an individual's make-up, and are <u>difficult to change</u>. Soft skills also include **[187]** <u>coping skills when faced with difficult situations and challenges</u>… <u>Again</u>, performance in these areas is linked with <u>inbuilt traits</u>.

INTERVIEWER: I see, and what about interpersonal skills, can't these be improved with practice or training?

MANAGER: Yes they can, because <u>it is possible to change the way that you interact with colleagues and customers</u>. The ability to **[188]** communicate effectively, both <u>through speech and in your documentation</u> is at the core of interpersonal skills. Equally **[189]** important is the ability to demonstrate respectful <u>listening</u>.

INTERVIEWER: And how will good soft skills help you in an interview situation?

MANAGER: **[190]** Soft skills are <u>vital</u> to a successful interview. The impression you create can play a <u>large part</u> in the decision to make a job offer, or not. Employers <u>need to know</u> that you have the right attitude. Will you fit in? Are you a team player? <u>Do you appear positive and enthusiastic</u>? <u>You must be able to make the necessary changes</u> to market yourself in this way.

INTERVIEWER: Well, thanks Mike. That's er… That's most interesting.

Section 4

Today I'm going to talk about a man who explained how life on earth evolved through a process of natural selection; the survival of the fittest.

[Q191] <u>His name is Charles Darwin and he was born in England in 1809</u>. Darwin's mother was the daughter of the renowned Staffordshire potter Josiah Wedgwood, and his father was a wealthy doctor. Darwin's mother died when he was nine years old, and his father sent him to boarding school. <u>During</u>

[Q192] <u>vacations, Darwin would collect and study wildlife, especially insects. In 1825</u>, Darwin attended the University of Edinburgh to study medicine. However, he lacked the aptitude for the subject, being more interested in botany. He joined a student natural history group, which introduced him

[Q193] to the science of geology. <u>Darwin left medical school two years later</u> without completing his training. Darwin's father was disappointed by his son's failure at Edinburgh and he sent him to Cambridge to study theology. He graduated from Cambridge in 1831, age 22, but decided against becoming a clergy-man, much to the dismay of his father. Whilst at Cambridge, Darwin had met a Professor of Botany who encouraged him to pursue his interest in natural history, and later recommended him as a crew member on the Royal Navy

[Q194] mapping ship, HMS *Beagle*. <u>The ship embarked for South America in 1831, sailing from Plymouth, England</u>. It dropped anchor in Brazil, Argentina, the Falkland Islands and Chile, before arriving at the Galapagos Islands in 1835. Here Darwin observed species of plants, birds and reptiles that were unique to the islands. The rest of the journey took in Sydney, Australia, and Cape Town, South Africa, with stops in the Keeling Islands and Mauritius. The route back to England included a stop in the tropics of South America, where Darwin made further important discoveries. The journey took five years and enabled Darwin to study life on three continents; collecting plants, insects

[Q195] and rock samples whilst <u>taking notes and making drawings</u>.

In 1839 Darwin married his cousin Emma Wedgwood, and they had 10

[Q196] children. <u>He published the zoological findings of the HMS *Beagle* expedition between 1838 and 1843</u>, in several parts covering birds, fossils, insects, reptiles and mammals. Darwin continued with his research into natural selection, culminating in his <u>seminal work</u> *On the Origin of Species*, <u>published in 1859</u>. <u>The book</u> was an overnight success, though it

[Q197] <u>caused widespread controversy</u> because its theories appeared to conflict with the accepted religious view of Creationism. Nevertheless, Charles Darwin's theories gradually gained acceptance, and when he died in 1882, age 73, he was honoured by being buried in Westminster Abbey. He will always be known as the father of evolution.

- -

Of all the places Darwin visited, it is the Galapagos Islands that are most associated with his theory of evolution. The islands lie in the Pacific Ocean off the coast of Ecuador, South America. The word galapago is Spanish for

[Q198] terrapin, and it refers to a <u>small edible turtle that Spanish sailors used as a food source</u>. Darwin observed variations in turtles, reptiles, birds and other species unique to each island, suggesting that the animals had adapted to their specific environment. The distances between the islands were too large for the animals to interbreed, so they must have descended from a common ancestor. <u>Darwin also found fossilized remains of creatures</u> that were now

[Q199] extinct, <u>consistent with a failure to adapt</u> to changes in habitat. Darwin believed in 'the survival of the fittest', that is to say only those members of a species that were best adapted to their surroundings would survive. For example, the finches on the islands had beaks of a different size and shape suited to their diet: long, pointed beaks to probe for grubs and to grab small seeds, or wider, sturdy beaks for cracking nuts and eating larger seeds.

[Q200] <u>The extinction of animals</u> not capable of competing for the food is vital to <u>Darwin's theory of natural selection</u>.

Test 4

Section 1

LIBRARIAN: Hi! Are you here for a library card?

STUDENT: Yes. What do I need to do?

LIBRARIAN: **[Q241]** I need to see proof of identity and <u>proof of residence</u>. You can use a driver's licence, a passport, a utility contract with your name and address on, or a tenancy agreement. Do you have any of those with you today?

STUDENT: **[Q242]** I have my passport and a copy of my <u>landlord's lease agreement</u>. Will they do?

LIBRARIAN: Let me see. You need to fill out this form whilst I check your ID.

STUDENT: It says here that I need a Personal Identification Number to access my account.

LIBRARIAN: **[Q243]** You can choose your own PIN. Make it a <u>four-digit number</u>, but not consecutive numbers like 1234 and you can't repeat a digit.

STUDENT: I'd like to take out some books today. Will that be possible?

LIBRARIAN: Once I've given you a valid library card and your PIN's been accepted.

STUDENT: Do I need to sign anywhere?

LIBRARIAN: Sign the bottom of the form and also the back of the card once I've finished with it. Have you included your e-mail address? We need this to notify you on your reserves and overdue items. We also e-mail a **[Q244]** monthly newsletter that includes details of <u>new titles</u>.

STUDENT: Can I access my account online?

LIBRARIAN: That's right. Just login with your library card number, shown beneath the **[Q245]** <u>bar code</u> and enter your PIN

STUDENT: What happens if I lose my card?

LIBRARIAN: We'll cancel your old card and issue you with a replacement for a fee of one dollar. The first card is free. You'll also need a new PIN. We don't e-mail it so you'll have to come in so we can reset it.

STUDENT: OK, thanks. Am I ready to start checking out materials now?

LIBRARIAN: Yes. You can access the library catalogue and your account right away. Here's a brochure telling you more about the library's lending policies and rules, as well as opening times, and there's information about late fees and lost items.

STUDENT: OK, I'm ready to take out a few items but can I go over a few things with you first please?

LIBRARIAN: What would you like to know?

STUDENT: Is there a limit on the number of items I can check out?

LIBRARIAN: **[Q246]** You can have <u>50 items</u> out at any one time, including a maximum of 10 DVDs and 5 CDs.

STUDENT: Wow that's quite a lot. What about how long I can take things out for; books for example?

. LIBRARIAN: The loan period is three weeks for books, unless they're new titles, in **[Q247]** which case it's <u>two weeks</u>. Magazines can be loaned for 10 days. DVDs for seven days.

STUDENT: **[Q248]** And are CDs <u>one week</u> the same as DVDs?

LIBRARIAN: <u>That's correct</u>.

STUDENT: What about renewals. How do I go about renewing items?

LIBRARIAN: You can renew items in several ways: either online by accessing your library account, or in person. You can also use our automated telephone renewal service or you can call the checkout desk.

STUDENT: And how many items can I renew?

LIBRARIAN: You can renew 10 items 4 days into their loan period.

STUDENT: I'm going to be working on a research project. I might need to reserve items that are currently out on loan. How do I go about doing this?

LIBRARIAN: It's through your library account. We'll e-mail you once the items are **[Q249]** available. You then have <u>five days</u> to pick them up before they go back into general circulation.

STUDENT: And can I just go on the computers when I come in or do I need to book a slot?

LIBRARIAN: **[Q250]** Yes, I'm glad you asked me that. We have <u>wireless laptops</u> for in-library use that can be borrowed for up to one hour. It's first-come first-served so <u>you cannot reserve these</u>. Alternatively, you can bring in your own laptop and log in to the library's home page using your library card number and PIN.

STUDENT: OK, that's great. Thanks for you help.

Section 2

Good afternoon rail passengers. The train arriving at Platform 4 is the overnight Express to Telstar city. This is our high speed, non-stop service

[Q251] with dining facilities and a sleeping car. The train will depart at <u>15.50 hours</u>. All passengers, including children, are required to have a boarding pass before they can board the train.

Please exchange your ticket for a boarding pass at the green booth <u>near the</u>

[Q252] <u>main entrance</u>. When you have obtained your boarding pass you can access Platform 4 through gate R. Passengers without tickets should obtain them from the manned ticket office at the Northgate Entrance, or use the self-

[Q253] service <u>ticketing machines located throughout the main hall</u>.

Passengers who <u>purchased their tickets online</u> and printed off a bar-coded

[Q254] boarding pass can access platform 4 <u>through gate T</u>, where their passes will be checked prior to boarding.

[Q255] Boarding will begin at approximately <u>15.05 hours</u>.

Please board the class of carriage shown on your boarding pass – <u>either</u>

[Q256] <u>standard class or premium class</u>. Your seat number is indicated on the pass. Reserved seats should be claimed at least 30 minutes before the

[Q257] train is due to depart. Reserved seats <u>not claimed by 15.20 hours</u> will be made available to other passengers.

If you have reserved a place in the sleeping car, please show your boarding pass to the attendant on the train, who will direct you to your sleeping compartment. Thank you.

- -

Welcome aboard the overnight express service to Telstar city. Meals are now being served on the train. Passengers travelling in Standard class can have a light meal in the dining car, located in the middle of the train, or bring their food back to their seats.

[Q258] <u>A limited selection of meals</u> is available from around 5 Euros.
Passengers travelling in Premium class can have their complimentary three-

[Q259] course <u>dinner and drinks</u> served in the dining car, or at their seat by the waiter. A full selection of meals is offered. This service is also available to sleeping-class passengers.

[Q260] Passengers in the sleeping car have a 5-star continental <u>breakfast included in the price,</u> and they can purchase additional drinks and snacks from the attendant. Thank you.

Section 3

INTERVIEWER: Good evening. Tonight we're taking a look at home composting. And here to tell us all about it we have in the studio Dr Marian Rotenberg, a soil scientist from the Institute of Environmental Integrity. Good evening, Dr Rotenberg.

DOCTOR: Good evening.

INTERVIEWER: Tell me. <u>Why is home composting such a hot topic at the moment</u>?

DOCTOR: Well, we need to recycle more of our domestic waste because **[Q261]** we're rapidly running out of landfill space, but <u>primarily it's to cut down on harmful greenhouse gases</u>, emitted from landfill sites. Also, compost is the natural way to improve the fertility of the soil for people interested in growing their own food, or organic gardening in general.

INTERVIEWER: Yes, I think most people understand the benefits of compost for the soil and also the landfill problem, but aren't greenhouse gases produced just the same when waste is left to decay in the garden?

DOCTOR: This is a common misconception. When waste is properly composted at home it generates far less greenhouse gases **[Q262]** than it would in a landfill site. There's also the <u>vehicle pollution to consider</u> when waste from millions of homes has to be transported to these sites.

INTERVIEWER: I realize that, but can you explain how home composting is preferable to decomposition in landfill?

DOCTOR: Well composting is a biological process that requires favourable conditions for microorganisms, mostly bacteria, to survive and multiply; that means sufficient oxygen, moisture, warmth and the correct acid/base balance. It's also important to use the correct **[Q263]** blend of organic materials, and to <u>agitate the compost to allow the air to circulate; this does not happen in landfill</u>.

INTERVIEWER: Er, yes. Many people are unsure as to exactly what is meant by 'organic materials' and what they can and cannot compost; can you give examples please?

DOCTOR: Well, <u>organic</u> means containing carbon, <u>but in composting</u> **[Q264]** <u>terms it refers to anything that was at one time living</u>. It can be divided into green material and brown material. The greens are kitchen scraps such as vegetable, salad and fruit waste, old flowers and grass clippings, these are a good nitrogen source. The browns include things like leaves, crushed eggshells, egg boxes, twigs and small branches, and shredded cardboard or paper, which provide the carbon.

INTERVIEWER: And do these browns and greens need to be mixed together?

DOCTOR: **[Q265]** <u>Normally it's more of a layering process</u>. Each layer of greens, that's food waste, is <u>covered by a layer</u> of browns; for example, leaves.

INTERVIEWER: Right, and are there any food substances that won't compost?

DOCTOR: Yes, most definitely. Don't add meat, fish, bones, dairy products or any kind of cooking oil because these are not very biodegradable and will slow the composting process down.

INTERVIEWER: Fine, I get the general idea. Thank you, that was most illuminating.

- -

INTERVIEWER: One of our listeners would like to know more about the practical aspects of home composting. Can you say more about this please?

DOCTOR: Yes, certainly. There's more than one method of composting but a **[Q266]** popular way is to use a ready-built <u>wooden frame, or a plastic composting bin</u> – made from recycled plastic of course; it can be sited anywhere in the garden, or placed near to the house for convenience if you wish. Ideally it should have a trapdoor at the bottom for access to the finished compost. The process **[Q267]** takes about <u>six to nine months</u>.

INTERVIEWER: That's quite long, isn't it.

DOCTOR: Yes, so it's often a good idea to have two composters, with a full one that can continue the process whilst you start the other bin. And one more thing, it's best to keep the kitchen scraps in a **[Q268]** <u>small plastic container with a sealed lid</u>; an old ice-cream carton <u>is suitable</u>.

INTERVIEWER: And how about the garden waste. Is that kept outside in another container?

DOCTOR: Yes, but it doesn't need to be a container with a lid, nothing **[Q269]** sophisticated. <u>Any enclosure in the garden will do. Just somewhere to keep leaves really</u>. Start with a layer of these at the bottom and then add a layer of kitchen scraps on a daily basis, topped off with another layer of leaves and twigs and so on, in roughly equal amounts.

INTERVIEWER: Now I know some people have concerns about attracting rodents and family pets. Is this really a problem?

DOCTOR: Well it can be, but it's less so if your bin has a lid or the kitchen scraps are well covered with leaves and twigs.

INTERVIEWER: And what <u>if there are not enough leaves</u> in your garden?

DOCTOR: <u>Crunched up newspaper and shredded card can provide an</u> **[Q270]** alternative source of carbon, and they also <u>increase the aeration of the compost</u>.

INTERVIEWER: Well, thank you once again, Doctor.

Section 4

Good morning. I'm Dr Mike Roberts, one of the institute's undergraduate tutors.... I'm going to talk briefly about the correct way to set out an academic essay, and also how to reference it. More details on submitting your essay and how to reference academic work generally, including research papers, can be found in the college handbook. That's the red book. You should all have a copy. These guidelines, or rules really, must be adhered to if you want to avoid losing marks. Five per cent of the total mark is available for correct referencing, which could mean the difference between a pass and a fail. OK, let's start with the page set-up. The margins should be one inch, each side, with one and a quarter inches at the top and bottom. Now, these are automatically chosen to suit the printer, so there's <u>no need to alter the</u>

[Q271] <u>normal template</u>. The text must be double-spaced to enable the tutor to add

[Q272] comments, either above or below the text, and also to <u>facilitate reading</u>. Choose a 12 point Times New Roman font for your essay – it must be typed

[Q273] and justified – <u>nothing is to be handwritten</u>, OK? Don't indent the paragraphs, and don't add additional blank lines between the paragraphs. It makes the essay look longer than it really is, but this will not fool the examiner. Now, <u>your essay will be marked and assessed anonymously</u>, to avoid any

[Q274] discrimination. So make sure that your <u>candidate number</u> appears in the right-hand corner of every page, in the top margin – the header – but <u>your name must not appear</u> anywhere on the final essay. Right, any questions so far? All this is in your handbook, by the way. I'll just mention the word count. To avoid being penalized <u>don't exceed the word count by more than 10 per cent.</u> So a 3,000 word essay shouldn't overrun by more than 300 words, or to put it another way, a 3,000 word essay should not be any longer

[Q275] than 3,300 words. <u>If you write any more words than this, the examiner is not obliged to read them.</u> Don't write anything less than 3,000 words though, OK?

Right, I'd like to move on to referencing. Well, why do we need to do it? ... Does anybody know? ... Firstly, citing references in an essay lends support to your own ideas and arguments; it's important to substantiate them. Secondly, in academic research, correct referencing enables other researchers

[Q276] to <u>locate the source of the material</u>, so that they can study it and check it. Finally, by acknowledging who wrote the work you cannot be accused of taking another author's ideas as being your own – which is plagiarism.

Now… some people might argue that there are no original ideas out there – that whatever you write, somebody else will already have written it – in which case you would end up having to reference all your written work. This

[Q277] is not true. <u>You do not have to reference facts that are well established and in the public domain</u>. So, for example, you can safely state that Sigmund Freud was the founder of psychiatry without having to reference it because it is a widely accepted fact; but what you cannot do is state that Freud was the first person to study the 'dreams of childhood', without quoting the relevant text… OK… I hope I've made that clear enough.

Now, we use the Harvard System of referencing here; its an author–date system. So <u>in the body of the essay</u> you would write, in parenthesis, the

[Q278] <u>author's surname, without the first name</u>, followed by a comma, followed by the date of the source. For example, Freud was the first person to study 'childhood dreams'; open brackets, Freud comma 1906, close brackets. OK?

[Q279] <u>When compiling your reference list, it should be placed in alphabetical order</u>, with the author's surname, initial, followed by the year of publication in

[Q280] brackets, then the title – which should be underlined – and <u>finally the city where the book was published along with the publisher's name</u>. For example: Freud, S, 1920, <u>A General Introduction to Psychoanalysis</u>, New York, Boni and Liveright. OK, that's it. Please refer to your red book for more details.

Answers

Marking scheme

There are 40 marks available for the Listening Test and 40 marks available for the Reading Test. You need at least 30 correct answers for every 40 questions, in other words no more than 10 wrong answers per test. If you achieve a minimum of 30 marks you should be ready to sit the IELTS test as long as you have kept to the time limits. If you score less than 30 out of 40 you need more practice. Academic candidates who fall short of 30 marks can attempt the General Training exercises for additional practice.

The table below shows approximately how many marks you need to score in the real IELTS for the Band Score indicated. General Training Candidates have to score higher marks in the Reading and Writing to achieve the same Band Score as Academic candidates in Reading and Writing. The table shows only full Band scores, but it is possible to be awarded half Band scores such as 6.5 and 7.5.

TABLE 7.1

	Band 5	Band 6	Band 7	Band 8
Listening Test marks and Academic Reading and Writing Test marks	16 to 22	23 to 29	30 to 34	35 to 38
General Training Reading and Writing Test marks	23 to 29	30 to 33	34 to 37	38 to 39

Test 1

Listening section

Section 1, Questions 1 to 10.

1   40 weeks

2   deposit

3   4 weeks

4   breakfast

5   dinner

6   Li

7   M24 7AB

8   0161 343651

9   no fish

10   2

Section 2, Questions 11 to 20.

11   Arts (Centre)

12   Sports (Hall)

13   Reed dining (room)

14   Information (Services)

15   Union shop

16   car park

17   Education centre

18   Moore (Hall)

19   Hepworth (Hall)

20   North (Road)

Section 3, Questions 21 to 30.

21   A

22   C

23   A

24   B

25   C

26, **27** and **28**   BDG

29   instruments

30   candidates

Section 4, Questions 31 to 40.

31   confusion

32   clouds

33   east

34   25

35   earth

36   Asia

37   65

38   position

39   male and female

40   several

Academic reading

Reading Passage 1, Questions 41 to 53.

Shedding light on it

41 TRUE

42 FALSE

43 NOT GIVEN

44 TRUE

45 FALSE

46 NOT GIVEN

47 TRUE

48 carbon footprint

49 warm

50 insulated

51 cold

52 mercury

53 efficient

Reading Passage 2, Questions 54 to 66.

Taking soundings

54 B

55 A

56 D

57 E

58 B

59 major concern

60 training exercises

61 common sense

62 migration routes

63 navigation

64 predators

65 cannot

66 social

Reading Passage 3, Questions 67 to 80.
Oxbridge

67 D

68 A

69 B

70 C

71 TRUE

72 FALSE

73 NOT GIVEN

74 FALSE

75 TRUE

76 NOT GIVEN

77 I

78 D

79 H

80 G

Academic writing

The following writing-task answers have been written by the author. The method used is explained at the end of each task. There are no right or wrong answers but you must cover all parts of the question. Marks are lost for mistakes in grammar, punctuation and spelling, as well as repetition of words. A higher mark is awarded for well-constructed sentences that communicate a clear message using sufficient vocabulary.

Writing task 1

The graph shows the use of wood, coal, oil and gas for a period between the years 1800 and 2000. Only wood was used for fuel in 1800. The use of wood declined following the advent of coal. This decline continued in a steady fashion for the next 150 years and after 1950 there was negligible use of wood.

No coal was used in 1800 but its use increased rapidly over the next 100 years. By about 1925, coal and wood were used in equal amounts, after which time coal became the most popular fuel. Coal reached its peak around 1900 and then, like wood, it declined steadily, as oil and gas became more popular.

Oil came into use after 1900. Starting at a low level, the percentage of oil rose quickly over the next 50 years before levelling off after about 1970.

Gas came into use at the same time as oil, and although less popular at first, the use of gas grew steadily over the next 100 years to eventually match oil.

It can be seen that coal, oil and gas account for roughly one-third each of the fuel used in the year 2000. At this time, coal was in decline, oil use was holding steady and gas was continuing to climb.

Method

The first paragraph introduces the graph stating what it does, taking care not to copy the words in the question. It then describes the change (trend) in wood usage over time. The second paragraph describes the trend in coal usage over time. The third paragraph describes the trend in oil usage over time. The fourth paragraph describes the trend in gas usage over time. The final paragraph compares all the fuels for the most recent time.

Writing task 2

The electronic calculator is a very useful tool for carrying out basic calculations and it is hard to imagine anyone never having used one. They are ideal for adding up large columns of numbers quickly and reduce the chances of making a mistake. This does not mean that a calculator should be used for making every calculation. In some maths problems – for example, fractions – it is not possible to find the solution with a calculator. For this reason, pupils should be able to solve arithmetic problems either in their head or by writing the calculation down on paper.

If calculators are introduced in school too early, the pupils will not have developed their mental arithmetic skills. In a situation where a calculator is not available, the pupils will find that they are unable to solve the problem. Calculators can save time but this is not always more important than being able to work out the right answer unaided. In the real world it is important to have a good grasp of numbers, even for simple things like money.

I believe that calculators should be allowed in schools but only after the pupils can remember their multiplication tables and work out basic arithmetic problems. It is very important that pupils have competent number skills so that they can work out a wide range of mathematical problems. Calculators are not the answer to every problem and it is still possible to make a mistake if you press the wrong button. Mental arithmetic is particularly useful for checking if an answer makes sense. A calculator is not an alternative to pupils using their brains.

Method

The first paragraph expands on what has been said in the question and includes the advantages of calculators and also some limitations. The second paragraph focuses on why calculators should not be allowed in school before number skills have been mastered. The third paragraph is used for the writer's own opinion as expressed by the words 'I believe'. It also brings together the advantages and dis-advantages of calculator use so as to create a balanced argument.

Test 2

Listening section

Section 1, Questions 81 to 90.

81   Harry Potter

82   15th June

83   Chew

84   5

85   £50

86   23rd June

87   £7

88   5471 4710 2382 3900

89   M236YC

90   Jane

Section 2, Questions 91 to 100.

91   C

92   A

93   B

94   C

95   C

96   B

97   sea

98   park

99   rope

100   climbers

Section 3, Questions 101 to 110.

101 60

102 title

103 48

104 essay

105 50

106 web page

107 school book

108 Introduction

109 third

110 top corners

Section 4, Questions 111 to 120.

111 C

112 B

113 A

114 B

115 C

116 A

117 diagrams

118 box

119 followed

120 rectangles

Academic reading

Reading Passage 4, Questions 121 to 133.

Rosetta Stone

121 FALSE

122 TRUE

123 FALSE

124 FALSE

125 TRUE

126 NOT GIVEN

127 TRUE

128 FALSE

129 E

130 G

131 B

132 J

133 C

Reading Passage 5, Questions 134 to 147.

Tickled pink

134 TRUE

135 TRUE

136 NOT GIVEN

137 FALSE

138 TRUE

139 FALSE

140 Rosy Glow

141 ripens

142 Ruby Pink

143 pink area / pink colour

144 Pink Lady

145 B

146 D

147 C

Reading Passage 6, Questions 148 to 160.

Bubbly and burgers

148 D

149 A

150 B

151 A

152 TRUE

153 TRUE

154 FALSE

155 NOT GIVEN

156 negligible risk

157 alcohol

158 very similar names

159 a food service

160 not exclusive

Academic writing

The following writing-task answers have been written by the author. The method used is explained at the end of each task. There are no right or wrong answers but you must cover all parts of the question. Marks are lost for mistakes in grammar, punctuation and spelling, as well as repetition of words. A higher mark is awarded for well-constructed sentences that communicate a clear message using sufficient vocabulary.

Writing task 1

The pie charts compare home ownership and renting for 1985 and 2005 in percentage terms.

In 1985, privately owned homes were the most popular type of housing, accounting for 55%, or more than over half of all homes. The next largest sector was council rented homes, amounting to 33% or nearly one-third of homes. The remaining homes were mostly privately rented (10%) with a tiny fraction being social housing (2%).

Twenty years later, in 2005, the number of privately owned homes had risen to 73%, or almost three quarters of all homes. This was an increase of 23% compared with 1985. Much of the increase in private ownership can be explained by the decrease in council rented homes, which had dropped from 33% to 11%. The percentage of privately rented homes had remained unchanged at 10%. However, there were 5 million more homes in 2005 compared with 1985 so the number of rented homes had increased despite the same percentage. Social housing has increased three-fold from 2% in 1985 to 6% in 2005, but it remains the least popular type of housing.

Method
The first paragraph introduces the pie charts, taking care not to copy what has been said in the question. The second paragraph deals with the year 1985, taking the segments in turn, starting with the largest segment and finishing with the smallest segment. The third paragraph describes the changes that have taken place by 2005 (increase, decrease, etc) when compared with 1985, taking each segment in turn.

Writing task 2

I do not believe that unemployed people should be given money for doing nothing. However, I accept that some people are unable to work through disabilities or ill health, in which case welfare payments are appropriate. Other than these exceptions, I see no reason why benefit claimants should not be made to work for their money like everyone else has to.

There are many advantages to working. It can help the long-term unemployed get back into the routine of work. It is very easy to get out of the habit of getting up early in the morning and working from '9 to 5'. There are self-esteem and confidence issues to consider. Working provides people with a sense of purpose and self-worth. It is easy to become socially isolated if you are out of work, whereas working forces you to meet new people. You might find something that you like doing or even learn new skills. It also looks good on your CV if you have been working rather than doing nothing. I found permanent work after a period of voluntary work in a charity shop.

The disadvantages of being made to work centre on the type of work that is available. If you are a professional person then manual work may be unsuitable for you. To save money, some employers might use unemployed people to do work that should be done by an employee.

I think that making unemployed people do some work for their welfare payments is a good idea. However, the workers should have some choice in the work that they do and it needs to be organized properly so that the employers cannot exploit them.

Method
The first paragraph starts with the writer's own opinion ('I do not believe') as a way of introducing the issues raised in the first part of the question. The second paragraph deals with the advantages of making unemployed people take a job. The third paragraph covers the disadvantages of making unemployed taking a job. The fourth paragraph answers the final part of the question where the author restates his own view, linking it neatly back to the introduction.

Test 3

Listening section

Section 1, Questions 161 to 170.

161   electricity

162   river

163   groups

164   20

165   8

166   goodnightpark

167   September

168   9.30

169   100

170   200

Section 2, Questions 171 to 180.

171   light work

172   bamboo

173   5 (people)

174   litter picking

175   average

176   building walls

177   6

178   B

179   A

180   C

Section 3, Questions 181 to 190.

181 A

182 B

183 C

184 A

185 B

186 B

187 B

188 C

189 C

190 A

Section 4, Questions 191 to 200.

191 England

192 wildlife

193 1827

194 ship

195 notes

196 1838

197 controversy

198 food

199 adapt

200 animals

Academic reading

Reading Passage 7, Questions 201 to 214.

Recalling it

201 B

202 D

203 C

204 F

205 E

206 NOT GIVEN

207 FALSE

208 TRUE

209 FALSE

210 FALSE

211 B

212 A

213 D

214 C

Reading Passage 8, Questions 215 to 226.

Home-schooling

215 Section B iii) Problems at school

216 Section C ix) Parents as teachers

217 Section D v) Overcoming a weakness

218 Section E ii) Range of benefits

219 Section F viii) Shared responsibility

220 FALSE

221 TRUE

222 NOT GIVEN

223 TRUE

224 FALSE

225 FALSE

226 TRUE

Reading Passage 9, Questions 227 to 240.

Biofuels backlash

227 Section A ii) Fossil fuel replacements

228 Section B vi) Environmentally friendly

229 Section C viii) Adverse affects

230 Section D x) Thorough examination

231 Section E iv) The way forward

232 FALSE

233 TRUE

234 FALSE

235 NOT GIVEN

236 FALSE

237 G

238 C

239 J

240 H

Academic writing

The following writing-task answers have been written by the author. The method used is explained at the end of each task. There are no right or wrong answers but you must cover all parts of the question. Marks are lost for mistakes in grammar, punctuation and spelling, as well as repetition of words. A higher mark is awarded for well-constructed sentences that communicate a clear message using sufficient vocabulary.

Writing task 1

Comparing activities, we can see that e-mail is the most popular activity with users of all ages. At least 90% of people use the internet for e-mails.

Whilst 80% of teenagers play online games, this figure drops to 55% of people in their twenties and 36% of people in their thirties. Online gaming reaches a low of 20% with people in their fifties and then increases in popularity with older people.

Music and video downloads display a similar trend to internet games, but they are less popular in general and decline markedly with people over age 40. Only 6% of people over age 70 download music and videos.

Online travel reservations are made by over half of all people except for teenagers who do not book any travel over the internet. Travel reservations peak in the thirties age group, when almost three-quarters of people make reservations in this way.

Online purchases are made by approximately two-thirds of people, except for those at both ends of the age scale, where internet shopping is less popular. Searching for people online is done by between one-quarter and one-third of people depending on age, except for teenagers who make only three searches out of every 100.

Method

The first paragraph identifies the most popular internet activity across the age groups. The second paragraph deals with online games, comparing percentages across the age groups, describing trends. The third paragraph deals with music and videos, in a similar way, as does the fourth paragraph on travel reservations. The fifth paragraph begins with online purchases and ends with searching for people.

Writing task 2

I believe that eating fast food is making our society overweight. However, people can choose what type of food they eat so fast food is not entirely to blame.

People will gain weight if they eat too much food or if it has a high fat or sugar content. It should be possible to control your weight by avoiding convenience foods, biscuits and snacks, and by making healthy choices at mealtimes. A lack of exercise also encourages obesity as does a family history of putting on weight. People should take action to stop themselves from becoming obese; for example, by going on a diet or taking more exercise. A more active lifestyle will help people to burn off the extra calories.

Fast-food companies must take some blame for obesity in society because they often sell high-fat food in oversize portions. They should offer healthier alternatives and label their food with its calorie content. Ready-made meals are very popular but these are not always the healthiest choices. People should cook more of their own food so that they know what has gone into it.

I think that obesity in children is the fault of the parents. Children should not be exposed to unhealthy high-fat foods too early in life or be allowed to develop a 'sweet tooth'. A visit to a fast-food restaurant should be an occasional treat rather than a regular eating habit. It is also important that schools encourage healthy eating in children by providing tasty, healthy food at lunchtime. If young people can make the right nutritional choices then obesity will not be a problem for society. (270)

Method

In the first paragraph, the author deals with the first part of the question, stating an opinion ('I believe'), whilst being careful to address both sides of the argument. The second paragraph deals with the factors that are responsible for obesity and how to deal with them. No specialist knowledge is required. The third paragraph deals with obesity looked at as a fast-food problem. The fourth paragraph discusses childhood obesity and some of the reasons for it; for example, unhealthy eating habits. There is no mention of exercise being important for children, but this is still a comprehensive and well thought out answer.

Test 4

Listening section

Section 1, Questions 241 to 250.

241 residence

242 lease agreement

243 4 digit number

244 new titles

245 bar code

246 50

247 2 weeks

248 1 week (or 7 days)

249 5 days

250 (wireless) laptops

Section 2, Questions 251 to 260.

251 C

252 B

253 B

254 C

255 A

256 B

257 C

258 meals

259 dinner and drinks

260 (continental) breakfast

Section 3, Questions 261 to 270.

261 B

262 C

263 A

264 C

265 B

266 wood

267 9

268 lid

269 leaves

270 newspaper

Section 4, Questions 271 to 280.

271 template

272 reading

273 handwritten

274 number

275 read

276 source

277 facts

278 first

279 list

280 last

Academic reading

Reading Passage 10, Questions 281 to 292.

Hacked off

281 TRUE

282 FALSE

283 TRUE

284 NOT GIVEN

285 TRUE

286 FALSE

287 FALSE

288 A

289 C

290 B

291 C

292 C

Reading Passage 11, Questions 293 to 306.

Highlands and Islands

293 TRUE

294 FALSE

295 NOT GIVEN

296 TRUE

297 FALSE

298 TRUE

299 FALSE

300 A

301 D

302 B

303 A vii) Location

304 B iv) Landscape

305 C ii) Language and culture

306 D v) Population and economic activity

Reading Passage 12, Questions 307 to 320.

Dummy pills

307 C

308 B

309 A

310 D

311 TRUE

312 TRUE

313 FALSE

314 TRUE

315 NOT GIVEN

316 NOT GIVEN

317 H

318 A

319 F

320 J

Academic writing

The following writing task answers have been written by the author. The method used is explained at the end of each task. There are no right or wrong answers but you must cover all parts of the question. Marks are lost for mistakes in grammar, punctuation and spelling, as well as repetition of words. A higher mark is awarded for well-constructed sentences that communicate a clear message using sufficient vocabulary.

Writing task 1

The bar chart depicts four types of waste disposal in four towns.

Landfill was the most popular method of waste disposal in towns A and D. Town A used landfill for disposing of about three-quarters of its waste with the remaining quarter split between incineration, recycling and composting. Town D used landfill for disposing of almost half of its waste with most of the rest being incinerated.

Incineration was the most popular method of waste disposal in towns B and C. Town C disposed of more than half its waste by incineration with less than one-quarter going for recycling and even less still going for landfill and composting.

Recycling was the second least popular method of waste disposal. No town disposed of more than 25% of its waste by recycling and in the case of town A, it was less than 10%.

Composting was the least common method of waste disposal. No town disposed of more than 10% of its waste by compositing and town D hardly did any composting.

Method
The first sentence introduces the chart without copying from the question. The second paragraph deals with landfill because the longest bar is found under landfill. The third paragraph deals with incineration. The fourth paragraph deals with recycling. The fifth paragraph deals with composting.

Writing task 2

I do not believe that academic achievement equates with a successful life. Obtaining good grades at school is a separate issue from making the most of your life. However, it is hard to see how a person can have a rewarding career without a sound education and appropriate qualifications; for example, a degree.

Well-educated and well-qualified people have more opportunities in the workplace and are more likely to find a well-paid job or be promoted. The result is often more job satisfaction and a better lifestyle compared with people who lack qualifications. On the downside there can also be more responsibility and stress.

It is still possible to do well in life without good qualifications. Not everybody is academically inclined. Many successful people left school at an early age and went on to achieve great things, often in the world of business. What is clear, though, is that most people had to work hard to achieve success, so failure to do well at school is not a good sign if it means that you were lazy.

There is more to life than work and money, so it is important to strike an appropriate work–life balance. Too much time spent working can harm people's social lives and relationships. Young people can lose out if they spend too much time studying rather than engaging in social activities and acquiring life skills.

I am not certain that by studying hard I will definitely improve my chances in life, but I am sure that I need to study if I am serious about wanting to improve myself. Good results in my examination alone will not bring success. I will have to make the most of my education and any opportunities that present themselves if I am to succeed.

Method

The author starts with his own opinion, whilst being careful to mention the other side of the argument so as not to appear biased (balanced view). The second paragraph looks at the advantages of having a good education (second part of the question) and also mentions a downside. The third paragraph explains that qualifications are not always needed to achieve success. The fourth paragraph explains some disadvantages of working too hard. The fifth paragraph deals with the last part of the question, pulling together strands from earlier paragraphs to provide a well thought out conclusion.

General Training

Test A

Reading section (A)
Section 1

Check-in procedure at Stanza Airport

321 FALSE

322 TRUE

323 FALSE

324 TRUE

325 NOT GIVEN

326 FALSE

327 NOT GIVEN

You're fired!

328 reason

329 wages

330 dismissal procedures

331 just cause

332 written down

333 gross misconduct

334 sacked

Section 2

Newview Hotel

335 (via the) website

336 breakfast

337 100%

338 (the) deposit

339 14.00 hrs

340 (the) room holder

A proper brew

341 wastes energy

342 set out

343 brewing process

344 properly infused

345 work surface

346 desired strength

347 prefer

Section 3

Vertical transport

348 FALSE

349 TRUE

350 TRUE

351 FALSE

352 TRUE

353 1854

354 1961

355 1903

356 1941

357 E

358 A

359 I

360 H

Writing section (A)

The following writing-task answers have been written by the author. The method used is explained at the end of each task. There are no right or wrong answers but you must cover all parts of the question. Marks are lost for mistakes in grammar, punctuation and spelling, as well as repetition of words. A higher mark is awarded for well-constructed sentences that communicate a clear message using sufficient vocabulary.

Writing task 1 Sample answer

Dear David

Thanks for writing. It's good to hear from you again and I hope you are well.

My preparation for the IELTS is going OK but I don't have enough time for studying. I am too tired in the evenings after a full day in the office, so I have to rely on the weekends. I might need to book some private lessons if I want a good score.

One thing I like to do is to read magazines in English whilst I travel to work on the train. This is helping me with my vocabulary and grammar. I also send out e-mails in English to practise for the writing section. When I get home I like to watch a film in English, with the subtitles turned off. My listening skills have improved greatly since I started watching films, which is more interesting than listening to CDs.

The most difficult section for me is the writing section because my grammar is not good enough. I am trying my best to learn the rules of English but some of the verbs seem to have more than one meaning and this is causing me trouble. I hope to sit the test in about three months.

Best wishes

Behnaz

Method
The writer introduces herself and thanks the reader for writing. The three paragraphs that follow deal with each of the bulleted points in turn. The first paragraph explains the author's progress in her IELTS preparation. The second paragraph outlines how the author is preparing for the test, by way of an example. The third paragraph covers the most difficult section for the author, again with examples.

Writing task 2 *Sample answer*

Many students choose to take a year out before going to university. To do so can be a positive and rewarding experience but there are also downsides to consider.

Some people will spend their time travelling whilst others will seek work experience. Travelling, especially to foreign countries, is advantageous because it broadens your outlook on life and its possibilities. It will make you more aware of different cultures and people and should increase your confidence, especially in social situations.

If you choose to spend your year out working this can also bring benefits. Work experience can help you to confirm that you have made the right degree choice. Working in an area related to your degree can also be helpful when it comes to finding a permanent job at the end of your course. A job can also improve your financial situation.

However, there are downsides to delaying your entry into university. One obvious problem is that you will have grown out of the habit of studying. There is a risk that the lure of paid employment will sway you from going to university altogether. If you spent your year out travelling then a future employer might look less favourably on you than a candidate who spent their time working.

I believe that a gap year can be a good idea as long as you do something productive that will be to your advantage in the future. Taking a year out can give you a better feel for life in the world in general and also in the workplace. You may never have the opportunity to take time out again so I would recommend it, but only if you choose carefully what to do or where to go.

Test B

Reading section (B)

Section 1

Use the right type of fire extinguisher!

361 TRUE

362 TRUE

363 NOT GIVEN

364 TRUE

365 FALSE

366 TRUE

367 TRUE

Contract of employment

368 viii

369 v

370 i

371 iv

372 ix

373 ii

374 vi

Section 2

How to create a blog

375 blogging service

376 guest users

377 dialogue boxes

378 text

379 interest

380 delete

Print, copy and scan

381 A

382 C

383 D

384 A

385 B

386 B

387 C

Section 3

Can an old dog learn new tricks?

388 FALSE

389 TRUE

390 TRUE

391 FALSE

392 NOT GIVEN

393 D

394 A

395 B

396 C

397 to **400**   H D B E (any order)

Writing section (B)

The following writing-task answers have been written by the author. The method used is explained at the end of each task. There are no right or wrong answers but you must cover all parts of the question. Marks are lost for mistakes in grammar, punctuation and spelling, as well as repetition of words. A higher mark is awarded for well-constructed sentences that communicate a clear message using sufficient vocabulary.

Writing task 1 Sample answer

Dear Sir/Madam

My name is Christopher Thompson and I am a new internet customer. On Monday I purchased a DVD player from your online shop with a view to playing MP3 discs, CDs and DVDs only to find that it will not play MP3 discs.

The web page stated that the DVD player was a new model capable of playing MP3 discs but this is clearly not the case. I have tried to play MP3 discs but was unable to do so. The user manual states quite clearly that it will only play CDs and DVDs and not MP3 discs.

I wish to exchange the model for one that will play MP3 discs. I do not wish to spend any more money so the replacement model must not be more expensive. If you do not have a suitable replacement, then please contact me by e-mail so I can return the item for a full refund, including postage and packaging costs. Please let me know your postal address for returns.

I look forward to your early response by e-mail, and I trust that you will update your web page so that it contains the correct information.

Yours faithfully

Christopher Thompson

Method
The letter deals with each of the three bulleted points in turn. The author introduces himself in the first paragraph, and then states briefly what the problem is (what the letter is about). The second paragraph explains the problem in more detail. The third paragraph states clearly what the author wants the shop to do. The final paragraph

covers how and when the author expects a reply, and makes a suggestion about how a similar problem can be avoided in the future.

Writing task 2 Sample answer

There are arguments both for and against children having to wear a school uniform. Some people favour uniforms simply because they look smart. However, uniforms do more than this because they identify you with a particular school which can help to maintain discipline and reduce truancy. Uniforms also promote safety and security by making it easier to identify intruders in the school. On a practical note, a uniform makes choosing clothes straightforward and problem-free for parents. Contrast this with the difficulties faced by parents with limited means (for example, living off state benefits) when a child wants to wear expensive designer clothes, mainly to impress friends. In this circumstance, children from poorer backgrounds can find themselves disadvantaged.

On the other hand, some people would argue that wearing a school uniform is an unnecessary restriction on personal freedom and expression. Instead, pupils should be allowed to choose their own clothes as suits them as individuals, rather than having to conform to a fixed dress code. Many pupils do not like a school uniform that means wearing the same clothes every day.

Personally I see nothing wrong with wearing a uniform to school because there is plenty of opportunity to wear your own clothes outside the school gates. Also, some restrictions are always necessary to stop people from dressing inappropriately whilst at school. There are strict dress codes and uniforms for adults in certain occupations so children might as well get used to the idea of having to wear a uniform of some type. I do not think it is a good idea to let young people have everything their own way too soon otherwise they will have problems with authority later on. (260)

Method

In the first paragraph, the author introduces the topic without copying from the question and then continues by explaining the benefits of wearing a school uniform. The second paragraph describes some disadvantages of wearing uniforms. The third paragraph covers the author's personal opinion on the topic, as required by the question, and includes more reasons to support the author's conclusion.

Reading section expanded answers

Reading Passage 1. Shedding light on it

Q41 (second paragraph) **TRUE. Incandescent bulbs convert more energy to heat than light. The statement is true because** *'converting less than 10% of the energy into light with the rest as heat' means more energy converted to heat than light (more than 90%).* A traditional light bulb is an incandescent bulb as described in the first sentence of the second paragraph.

Q42 (third paragraph) **FALSE. Ultraviolet light (UV) can be seen with the naked eye. The statement is false because** *'this light is invisible',* referring to the ultraviolet (UV) light, means that it cannot be seen with the naked eye. (Q42 – trick. You may be tricked into answering TRUE. The word 'visible' applies to white light not to UV light.)

Q43 (third paragraph) **NOT GIVEN. Compact fluorescent lamps (CFLs) last about 10 years.** There is no information on the lifespan of CFLs in the passage. We cannot say whether it is true or false. (Q43 – trick. 'ten times the life expectancy' does not mean lasting 10 years.)

Q44 (fourth paragraph) **TRUE. Fluorescent tubes are the best light for work-places.** The answer is true because *'The bright light produced by standard fluorescent lights makes them an ideal choice for offices and factories'*. True because *'ideal'* means 'best'; and 'offices and factories' are 'workplaces'.

Q45 (fifth paragraph) **FALSE. Incandescent bulbs contain mercury.** The answer is false because *'Traditional bulbs… are free from mercury'*, means that they do not contain any mercury, noting that an incandescent bulb is a traditional bulb.

Q46 (fifth paragraph) **NOT GIVEN. Fluorescent light can cause headaches and migraines.** There is no information on fluorescent lighting triggering headaches and migraines in the passage. We cannot say whether it is true or false based on the information in the passage. (Q46 – trick. 'can cause eye strain' is not the same as headaches and migraines.)

Q47 (sixth paragraph) **TRUE. Traditional bulbs may waste less energy than they appear to.** The answer is true because *'this heat is not wasted'*.

Q48 (sixth paragraph) **carbon footprint**. The answer is *'carbon footprint'* because *'reduced carbon footprint'* means the same as smaller carbon footprint. (Q48 distracter: the phrase *'Whilst it is true'* distracts the reader into thinking the answer must come after this phrase, whereas the answer is found in the previous sentence.)

Q49 (sixth paragraph) **warm**. The answer is *warm* because *'The bulb helps to keep the house warm'*.

Q50 (sixth paragraph) **insulated**. The answer is *insulated* because *'the savings are less than expected in well (insulated) homes'* means the same as *'save less energy than you might imagine if your home is properly insulated'*, noting the links between 'properly' and 'well', and also 'save less energy than you might imagine' and 'the savings are less than expected'.

Q51 (sixth paragraph) **cold**. The answer is *cold* because *'cold regions'* in the summary means the same as *cold climate* in the passage.

Q52 (fifth paragraph) **mercury**. The answer is *mercury* because *'hazardous for health'* in the summary can be linked to *'Mercury can accumulate in the body to attack the brain and central nervous system'*.

Q53   (seventh paragraph) **efficient**. The answer is _efficient_ because _'more efficient'_ in the summary following on from the words 'though expensive' can be linked to _'twice as efficient'_ in the passage.

Reading Passage 2. Taking soundings

Q54   Paragraph **B. an example of sound being used other than for navigation and location of prey**. _Communication_ is the other use, as described in the first sentence of paragraph B.

Q55   Paragraph **A. examples of mammals other than whales and dolphins that use echolation**. Bats are the other mammal as described in the first sentence of passage A.

Q56   Paragraph **D. how man's behaviour has increased the number of whales being stranded**. '_high-power military sonar_ might disorientate or harm whales, and that it is _responsible for_ the mass _strandings_ seen on beaches'.

Q57   Paragraph **E. an example of whales living in a community**. 'Whales are social animals _that swim in groups known as "pods"_.'

Q58   Paragraph **B. why people cannot hear whale song**. '_Low frequency vocalizations, in the form of grunts and moans are inaudible to the human ear, but form a pattern or song_'. (Q58 distracter: the clicks, known as ultrasound, consist of high pitch (frequency) sound waves, '_well above the range of the human ear, and distinct from the low pitched whale song_').

Q59   **major concern** (paragraph D). The answer is _'major concern'_ **because the first sentence of paragraph D** includes the key words, harm, sonar and major concern, which are found in the summary in reverse order.

Q60   **training exercise** (paragraph D). The answer is _'training exercise'_ **because the phrase** _'number of beachings have been seen to increase'_, in the summary is the same as _'stranding occurs more frequently'_ in the passage.

Q61   **common sense** (paragraph D). The answer is _'common sense'_ **because** _'the impact of sonar on mammals can be lessened'_ can be likened to _'take steps to minimize the effects of sonar on mammals'_ wherever possible. Most of _these_ precautions _are common sense_.

Q62   **migration routes** (paragraph D). The answer is *'migration routes'* **because** *'keep away from migration routes'* fits with *'avoiding whale migration routes'*.

Q63   **navigation** (paragraph E). The answer is *'navigation'* **because** *'mistakes in navigation'* are *'navigation errors'*, and *'changes in the earth's magnetic compass'* is the same as *'fluctuations in the earth's magnetic field'*.

Q64   **predators** (paragraph E). The answer is *'predators'* **because the phrase** *'straying into shallow water'* appears in both the summary and the passage and *'perused by'* fits with *'attempting to escape'*.

Q65   **cannot** (paragraph E). The answer is *'cannot'* **because** 'When a single whale is found dead on a beach it might have died from *natural causes* out at sea.... It is apparent that multiple deaths at sea *cannot* produce a "mass stranding"', that is to say a *group of whales* cannot.

Q66   **social** (paragraph E). The answer is *'social'* **because** *swim into shallow water as a group* is the same as *'swim in groups known as "pods"'*.

Reading Passage 3. Oxbridge

Q67   **D.** (first paragraph) *'In the past Oxbridge* has been seen as **a place that represents the highest educational standards**'. This answer is reflected in *'Traditionally, a degree at Oxbridge symbolized the pinnacle of academic achievement.'*

Q68   **A.** (second paragraph) *'Everybody agrees that **too many Oxbridge students have had a private education**.'* This answer is reflected in *'It cannot be disputed that a disproportionate number of Oxbridge entrants went to a fee-paying private school rather than to a free, state school.'* (Q68 distracter: *Some people believe* that Oxbridge is part of a social class system that favours the privileged few.)

Q69   **B.** (third paragraph) 'In the passage, there is an example of how Oxbridge has **made the application process fairer**'. This answer is reflected in 'Indeed, in some subjects *the application process* includes admissions and aptitude tests that help to ensure *a level playing field*.'

Q70 **C.** (second paragraph) 'In the passage, a *link* is made between a *degree at Oxbridge* and **a successful career**.' This answer is reflected in '*Oxbridge graduates* are *rewarded* with the *best-paying jobs.*'

Q71 **TRUE.** (third paragraph) **The 'Oxbridge advantage' refers to better prospects in life.** The statement is true because 'Oxbridge helps to maintain the "social divide" where the *rich get richer* and the poor remain poor. Some people would argue that *this "Oxbridge advantage"...*'.

Q72 **FALSE.** (third paragraph) **Some Oxbridge candidates are offered a place whether they deserve it or not.** The statement is false because There is *no evidence* to suggest that Oxbridge selects students on *anything other than merit*.

Q73 **NOT GIVEN.** (third paragraph) **A student from an ordinary background is unlikely to do well at Oxbridge.** There is no information on this in the passage. Whilst a student from an ordinary background is less likely to secure a place at Oxbridge, no information is given about how well they do once at Oxbridge. (Q73 distracter: some pupils from an *ordinary background* are *not comfortable* with the *idea of attending Oxbridge*; this says nothing about the student's performance at Oxbridge.)

Q74 **FALSE.** (third paragraph) **A lack of applications from state schools is the only reason for the low number of state school students at Oxbridge.** The answer is false because '*Alternatively, the low aspiration of some pupils' parents* may fail to drive gifted pupils onwards and upwards.' In other words, there is another reason (a second one). Q73 'distracter' offers a third possibility (a third alternative).

Q75 **TRUE.** (fourth paragraph) **The author does not believe that Oxbridge is responsible for social inequalities.** The answer is true because '*Inequalities* in our society *do not begin and end* with Oxbridge.'

Q76 **NOT GIVEN.** (fourth paragraph) **There are few good schools in the state sector.** There is no information given about the number of good state schools or the proportion of state schools that are good.

Q77 *Answer* **I. prosperous.** (fourth paragraph) The answer is 'prosperous' **because it means the same as** affluent in '*The best state schools tend to be found in the most **affluent** areas*'.

Q78   *Answer* **D. fairness**. (fourth paragraph) The answer is *'fairness'* **because** 'a lack of *fairness in* the state school system' summarizes '*Injustices* can arise when parents move house to secure a child's place at a more desirable school.'

Q79   *Answer* **H. privately**. (fourth paragraph) The answer is *'privately'* because 'pay for them to be educated privately' is the same as '*will pay for* their children to be educated at *a private school*.'

Q80   *Answer* **G. important**. (fourth paragraph) The answer is *'important'* **because** '*more important*' is the same as '*outweighs*'.

Reading Passage 4. Rosetta Stone

Q121   **FALSE.** (first paragraph) The Rosetta Stone was unearthed in the city of Alexandria. The statement is false because '*discovery was made in the small town of Rashid, 65 km from the city of Alexandria*'.

Q122   **TRUE.** (second paragraph) **There are three translations of the same passage on the Rosetta Stone.** The statement is false because 'it is carved with the same text *written in two* Ancient Egyptian *scripts* (hieroglyphics and Demotic) *and in Greek*.'

Q123   **FALSE.** (second paragraph) **Egyptian scholars wrote the passages almost 4,000 years ago.** The statement is false because 'The "Pierre de Rosette" *dates back to 196 BC*. (Q123 distracter: 'Egyptian hieroglyphs dating back almost 4,000 years', which does not refer to the words on the stone.)

Q124   **FALSE.** (third paragraph) **Thomas Young translated the entire Demotic test.** The statement is false because 'Thomas Young translated *some of the words in the Demotic section* of the stone.'

Q125   **TRUE.** (third paragraph) **The hieroglyphs were more difficult to translate than the Demotic text.** The statement is true because '*he made little headway with the hieroglyphics symbols, which proved baffling*'.

Q126   **NOT GIVEN. Demotic language used phonetic sounds.** There is no information given on phonetic sounds in relation to the demotic language.

(Q126 distracter: 'the symbols used a combination of alphabet letters and phonetic sounds', refers to the hieroglyphic symbols.)

Q127 **TRUE.** (third paragraph) **Jean-Francois Champollian is the founder of the science of Egyptology.** The statement is true because *'Champollian is acknowledged as the father of modern Egyptology.'*

Q128 **FALSE.** (fourth paragraph) **The Rosetta Stone was the only stone of its type.** The statement is false because *'The stone is not unique'*; there were similar stones.

Q129 **E.** (fifth paragraph) The head of Egypt's antiquities believes **that the country's treasured antiquities belong in Egypt**. The answer is reflected in 'In recent times, *Egypt's head of antiquities*, Dr Zahi Hawass, has *lobbied for the return* of the Rosetta Stone *to Egypt*, along with *other prized antiquities'*. Note that answer **A.** *all items* of cultural heritage is a distractor (Dr Hawass has not requested every item).

Q130 **G.** (fifth paragraph) The *return* of antiquities to their country of origin is a topic **that *provokes debate* and *generates strong feelings***. The answer is reflected in 'The *repatriation* of artefacts of cultural heritage is a *controversial and emotive issue*.'

Q131 **B.** (fifth paragraph) In 2002, 30 museums *stated* **that the *taking of antiquities* cannot be *judged* by today's standards**.The answer is reflected in 'the *joint declaration* that "*objects acquired in earlier times must be viewed in the light of different sensitivities and values reflective of that earlier era*"'.

Q132 **J.** (sixth paragraph) Where prized artefacts are concerned, there is a danger **that the borrowed items will be kept and not returned**. The answer is reflected in 'The British Museum *will loan treasured artefacts* to other museums around the world, though in doing so *it runs the risk of not getting them back'*.

Q133 **C.** (seventh paragraph) Rosetta Stone is a name **that is associated more with language training than with antiquities**. The answer is reflected in *'the term "Rosetta Stone" has been adopted by a language-learning* company and is *more likely to be recognized in this context than as an important cultural artefact.'*

Reading Passage 5. Tickled pink

Q134 **TRUE.** (second paragraph) **Pink Lady apples are the highest grade of Cripps Pink apples. The statement is true because** 'The highest-quality apples are marketed worldwide under the trademark Pink Lady™.'

Q135 **TRUE.** (third paragraph) **One advantage of Cripps Pink trees is that they grow well.**
The statement is true because 'its advantages… include vigorous trees'.

Q136 **NOT GIVEN. Cripps Pink trees produce an abundance of fruit.** There is no information on the quantity of fruit from the tree.

Q137 **FALSE.** (third paragraph) **Pink Lady apples are less expensive to buy than Cripps Pink apples. The statement is false because the** 'premium price that the Pink Lady brand is able to command' indicates that the Pink Lady is more expensive.

Q138 **TRUE.** (third and fourth paragraphs) *Colour* **is an important factor in the** *selection* **of both of the premium grades of Cripps apples referred to. The statement is true because** 'To earn the name Pink Lady the skin of a Cripps Pink apple must be at least 40% pink' and 'Apples that fall outside of this colour ratio are rejected.'

Q139 **FALSE.** (fourth paragraph) Lady Williams apples are sweeter than Golden Delicious. **The statement is false because** 'Both apples are sweeter than Lady Williams but neither is as sweet as Golden Delicious' where 'both apples' refers to Cripps Red and Cripps Pink. Order of sweetness. Golden delicious (most sweet) are sweeter than Cripps Red/Pink which are sweeter than Lady Williams (least sweet).

Q140 **Rosy Glow.** (fifth paragraph) The answer is 'Rosy Glow' **because** 'A bud taken from a mutated branch on a Cripps Pink Tree… to produce the new variety named Rosy Glow' can be likened to 'A bud was taken from the mutated branch to produce the new variety. The fruit from the new Rosy Glow tree….' The mutated branch is from a Cripps Pink tree.

Q141 **ripens.** (fifth paragraph) The answer is 'ripens' **because it** ripens sooner than the Pink Lady with less sun can be likened to 'it ripens earlier in the season in climates that have less hours of sunshine'.

Q142 **Ruby Pink.** (sixth paragraph) The answer is '*Ruby pink*' **because** *Ruby Pink and Lady in Red are two mutations of the Cripps Pink that were discovered in New Zealand*; a mutation is a strain. (Q142 distractor: Lady in Red is an incorrect answer because it contains three words.)

Q143 **pink area/pink colour.** (sixth paragraph) The answer is '*pink area*' (or pink colour) **because** 'The chief advantage of new and improved strains is that the apples develop more *pink area*' can be likened to '*improved varieties develop a larger area of pink* than the Cripps Pink'.

Q144 **Pink Lady.** (sixth paragraph) The answer is *'Pink Lady'* **because** 'so that more can use the name Pink Lady' can be likened to '*allows more apples to meet the quality requirements of the Pink Lady™* brand'.

Q145 **B. Sundowner™.** (fourth paragraph) The answer is *'Sundowner™'* **because** 'the trade mark of the *highest quality* Cripps Red apple' is reflected in '*The premium grade is marketed as the Sundowner™*' (fourth paragraph).

Q146 **D. Lady Williams.** (fourth paragraph) The answer is '*Lady Williams*' **because** '*both apples are sweeter than Lady Williams but neither is as sweet as Golden Delicious*' where 'both apples' refers to Cripps Red and Cripps pink. Lady Williams is the least sweet apple (see also Q139).

Q147 **C. mutation of a Cripps Pink tree.** (sixth paragraph) The answer is *Lady in Red* **because** '*Ruby Pink and Lady in Red are two mutations of the Cripps Pink*', noting that Ruby Pink is not in the list of possible answers.

Reading Passage 6. Bubbly and burgers

Q148 **D.** '*The passage "Bubbly and burgers" is mainly concerned with "the meaning of passing off".'* There is no single sentence that reflects this answer. You need to have read the entire text to make your choice, and in doing so, eliminate answers A, B and C. Answer A 'Champagne and McDonald's' might appear to be the right answer to someone who has not read the passage because it identifies with 'Bubbly and burgers' but the passage is concerned with 'passing off'; answer B '"copycat" food and drink' looks possible, but it places emphasis on food and drink as much as 'passing off'; answer C 'the impact of "passing off" on trade' is touched on in the first paragraph and occasionally later on, but it is not the main thrust of the passage, which is D, 'the meaning of passing off', which is explained *by way of examples* (Champagne, Advocaat, Vodka, burgers, coffee, etc).

Q149 **A.** (second paragraph) 'In the passage the author states that *sparkling wine 'is* **not Champagne** *unless it* **originates from** *the Champagne region'.* This answer is reflected in 'The Champagne growers of France have successfully *defended the Champagne brand* against any *sparkling* wine produced outside the Champagne region'. (Q149c is a distracter for the false answer C.)

Q150 **B.** (third paragraph) 'In the passage the author states that '*Elderflower champagne 'is* **similar to Champagne in the foam it produces**'. This statement is reflected in 'It self-ferments to *produce Champagne-like foam* when the bottle is opened'. Q150a is a distracter sentence for answers C and D; Q150b is a distracter sentence for answer A ('is a non-alcoholic Champagne' is very different to 'might believe it is non-alcoholic Champagne').

Q151 **A.** (fourth paragraph) 'The passage indicates that Norman McDonald '**falsely represented his business as a McDonalds franchise**'. This answer is reflected in 'He was forced to remove the arches... *so as not to misrepresent the business as a McDonald's franchise*. Note the distractors: he was not innocent (B), and he was forced to remove the golden arches, but not the name McDonalds, and two lit arches (C) were not stated to be indistinguishable (identical) to the McDonald's logo.

Q152 **TRUE.** (first paragraph) **Passing off and palming off are different breaches of civil law.** The statement is true **because** '*Unfair trading is a breach of civil law*' and '*In the UK, unfair trading is known as "passing off" and in the USA as "palming off"*'.

Q153 **TRUE.** (second paragraph) **Champagne production involves two fermentation processes.** The statement is true **because** 'the fizz is obtained via a *secondary fermentation* process...'.

Q154 **FALSE.** (second paragraph) *Inexpensive* **sparkling wines are carbonated** *naturally inside the bottle*. The statement is false **because** 'In a *budget sparkling wine*, the fizz is generated *artificially* by injecting high pressure carbon-dioxide gas into still wine *prior to bottling*, as per carbonated drinks.

Q155   **NOT GIVEN.** 'Elderflower "Champagne" is a popular summer drink in several EU countries' is not the same as 'Elderflower "Champagne" is a *favourite non-alcoholic summer drink in the UK*', **because** no reference is made to any other EU countries.

Q156   **negligible risk.** (third paragraph) The answer is '*negligible risk*' **because** 'the judge *deemed that the risk of damage to the reputation* of genuine Champagne *was negligible*.

Q157   **alcohol.** (third paragraph) The answer is '*alcohol*' **because** 'Diageo… *prevented* Intercontinental Brands from selling… Vodkat, *primarily because it did not contain the necessary 37.5% alcohol.*'

Q158   **very similar names.** (fifth paragraph) The answer is '*very similar names*' **because of the phrase** '*including those with very similar names, such as MacDonald's and Mcdonald*'.

Q159   **a food service.** (fifth paragraph) The answer is '*a food service*' **because** 'they were more likely to **succeed** *if the defendants had* **a clear association** *with a food service*'.

Q160   **not exclusive.** (fifth paragraph) The answer is '*not exclusive*' **because** '*It was also* **indicated** *that McDonald's* **did not have exclusive rights** *to the prefix Mc*'.

Reading Passage 7. Recalling it

Q201   Paragraph **B**. **How early man benefited from stress.** '*In our* **primitive ancestors***, emotional* **stress** *had* **a survival value***.*'

Q202   Paragraph **D**. **How a person can reduce the effects of stress.** '*change your thoughts and emotional reactions to the stressor, so as* **to lessen its impact***.*'

Q203   Paragraph **C**. **How candidates fear examinations.** '*"Pre-exam nerves" is an anxiety state experienced by candidates prior to an examination. It is perfectly natural to* **feel apprehensive** *about an important test.*'

Q204   Paragraph **F. How a speaker can make a confident start.** *It is essential to make a **solid start**,* in which case it is advisable to **memorize the opening lines** of the speech.

Q205   Paragraph **E. How communication fails if important facts are out of order.** '***the message is lost** when **salient points** are either omitted or **out of sequence**.*'

Q206   **NOT GIVEN**. There is no information on whether our ancestors experienced higher levels of stress than we do today.

Q207   **FALSE**. (Paragraph C) **A 'retrieval failure' is a permanent loss of knowledge**. This statement is false **because** '*The knowledge has been **forgotten temporarily**'*.

Q208   **TRUE**. (Paragraph D) **Learning by rote is memorizing by repetition**. This statement is true **because** 'short-term memory improves if you **repeat new information to yourself several times, learning by rote**'.

Q209   **FALSE**. (Paragraph D) **Relaxation techniques can help a candidate to gain new knowledge**. This statement is false **because** '*Relaxation techniques* will improve the memory but they **cannot help** a candidate to retrieve **knowledge that they have yet to acquire**'.

Q210   **FALSE**. (Paragraph E) **Headings enable a complete image of an event to be recalled**. This statement is false **because** '*When information is classified under these headings it acts as a cue that **enables** the reader to construct **partial images** of previous events'.*

Q211   **B**. (Paragraph E) To recall **past events** from **notes** it is **helpful** '*to group information* under headings'. This statement is reflected in 'Accurate recall of past events is facilitated by note-taking and in particular by **placing information under the headings.**'

Q212   **A**. (Paragraph E) When revising for an examination it is helpful '*to use a range of memory aids*'. This statement is reflected in '*it is useful to include both visual and verbal aids when revising for an examination*'.

Q213   **D**. (Paragraph E) A mnemonic is '*a spelling revision aid*'. This statement is reflected in '*mnemonic devices… that aid spelling*'.

Q214 **C**. (Paragraph F) A slide **can help** a speaker 'to recall **essential informa-tion**'. This statement is reflected in '*Each slide* contains a few key elements *that serve to* cue the memory towards the *necessary detail*'.

Reading Passage 8. Home-schooling

Q215 Paragraph **B. iii)** The paragraph deals with 'Problems at school'. The key phrase is '*removed from a school following negative experiences*'.

Q216 Paragraph **C. ix)** The paragraph deals with 'Parents as teachers'. The word 'parents' is mentioned five times and the key phrase is '*Parents are not professional teachers*'. Answer i) 'Disadvantages' is a distracter linked to 'education in the home environment can have its limitations'.

Q217 Paragraph **D. v)** The paragraph deals with 'Overcoming a weakness' (lack of socialization) as indicated by '*Socialization outside of the home can negate some of these shortcomings*'. Answer i) 'Disadvantages' is a dis-tracter linked to 'the main criticism of home-schooling', noting that 'Main disadvantage' (one only) would fit with this paragraph.

Q218 Paragraph **E. ii)** The paragraph explains the 'Range of benefits' when referring to '<u>Whilst home-schooling has its shortcomings it also offers (Q218) *several advantages*</u>'. Answer iv) 'Main advantage' is a distracter, noting that the paragraph explains many advantages, not just one.

Q219 Paragraph **F. viii)** The paragraph explains the 'Shared responsibility' when referring to 'it is the *duty of the state and the parents*'.

Q220 **FALSE.** (Paragraph A) **In the USA there are four times as many home-educated children as in the UK**. This statement is false **because** '*In the UK… 100,000 pupils. In the USA… approximately two million children.*' Noting that the figures of 1% and 4% are distracters.

Q221 **TRUE**. (Paragraph A) **There is much disagreement about the merits of home-schooling**. This statement is true **because** '*Home-schooling is a controversial issue*'.

Q222 **NOT GIVEN. School children with disabilities are the most dis-criminated against**. Discrimination is referred to in paragraph B but not in relation to disabilities.

Q223   **TRUE**. (Paragraph C) **There is nothing unusual about children learning from their parents at home**. This statement is true **because** 'Whilst home-schooling of a child is unusual, *learning from parents is not.*'

Q224   **FALSE**. (Paragraph D) **Only children who attend school can be favourably socialized**. This statement is false because '*socialization experienced in the natural setting of a community is preferable to that within the confines of a school'*.

Q225   **FALSE**. (Paragraph E) **Pupils in school achieve higher grades than home-school children**. This statement is false because '*home-educated children usually outperform their schooled counterparts academically'*.

Q226   **TRUE**. (Paragraph E) **Children from better-off homes are more likely to complete their homework**. This statement is true because 'Parents who home-school their children tend to be… *in a higher… income bracket… more likely… encouraging compliance with homework.'*

Reading Passage 9. Biofuels backlash

Q227   Section **A. ii)** This section (paragraph) deals with 'Fossil fuel replacements'. The indicative words are '*alternative*' and '*replacement*'. Answer i) Biofuels is a distracter; we already know from the heading 'Biofuels backlash' that the passage deals with biofuels.

Q228   Section **B. vi)** This section explains why fuel crops are 'Environmentally friendly' stating that '*Energy crops offer one solution to the deleterious effects of carbon-dioxide emitted from vehicle exhausts. Biofuels are 100% carbon-neutral which means that there is no net gain or loss of carbon to the environment*' and later '*less atmospheric pollution as well as less global warming. Biofuels are less toxic than fossil fuels and biodegrade if spilt on the ground.'*

Q229   Section **C. viii)** This section deals with 'Adverse effects' citing three examples (firstly, secondly and thirdly).

Q230   Section **D. x)** This section refers to a 'Thorough examination' in the statement '*To judge whether or not biofuels are genuinely a greener alternative to fossil fuels it is necessary to* **scrutinize** *the manufacturing steps.'*

Q231 Section **E**. **iv)** This section covers 'The way forward', in particular when it uses the phrase '_Biodiesel consumption may, in the future_' but also with the additional term 'New technologies', and the phrases 'may be the answer' and 'can be developed'.

Q232 **FALSE.** (Paragraph A) **Bio-ethanol is a non-renewable fuel source.** This statement is false because '_Biodiesel and bio-ethanol are cleaner, sustainable alternatives_ to petroleum based fuels.'

Q233 **TRUE.** (Paragraph B) **Burning biodiesel instead of petroleum diesel generates less pollution.** This statement is true because (with reference to biodiesel) '_The latter burns more efficiently_ than petroleum diesel... which means _less atmospheric pollution._'

Q234 **FALSE.** (Paragraph C) **Food prices fall when fuel crops are planted on land used to grow food.** This statement is false because '_energy crops are planted on existing agricultural land, but if this is done it reduces the supply of food crops, creating **a surge** in food prices_'.

Q235 **NOT GIVEN. Fuel crops outnumber food crops in developing countries.** There is no information on fuel crops exceeding food crops, noting that 'have barely sufficient food to eat and switching to fuel crops could threaten their meagre food supplies (Paragraph C) is a distracter.

Q236 **FALSE.** (Paragraphs C and D) **The eco-friendly nature of biofuels cannot be disputed.** This statement is false because '_Not everybody believes that biofuels are the ideal alternative to fossil fuels. The status of biofuels as environmentally friendly can be **challenged** on several counts_', and '_Whilst in theory, the carbon released by biofuels is equivalent to that removed from the atmosphere by the growing plants this does not reflect the true energy picture._'

Q237 **G** (Paragraph D) _Excess fertilizer_ can be _deadly to fish_ **if it _drains_ into the _surrounding watercourses_**. The answer is reflected in '_surplus nitrates can leach into nearby rivers and streams where they kill the fish_'.

Q238 **C** (Paragraph E) The _green status_ of energy crops is _strengthened_ **if they are not planted on _agricultural land_**. The answer is reflected in 'To _reinforce_ their _green credentials_, energy crops _should not be planted on land that was being used to produce food._'

Q239 **J** (Paragraph E) It may not be necessary to acquire *more land* **if *yields are improved* with *genetically modified crops*.** The answer is reflected in '*Genetically modified plants* may be the answer to *increasing* biofuel *crop yields without* the need for further *land grab*.'

Q240 **H** (Paragraph E) Farmers in poorer countries will benefit from fuel crops **if they can keep the profits they make**. The answer is reflected in '*Developing countries* that grow biofuels *should be allowed to benefit* from the *premium prices* that fuel crops command, *enabling farmers* and their communities to *reap economic* and social *benefits*.'

Reading Passage 10. Hacked off

Q281 **TRUE**. (first paragraph) **Malware is usually downloaded from the internet by mistake**. True because '*Typically, these programs are downloaded from the internet **inadvertently**.*'

Q282 **FALSE**. (second paragraph) **An e-mail text can carry a virus.** False because '*The text portion of the e-mail cannot carry any malware.*' Q282 distractor: '*A virus can be released when a user opens an e-mail and downloads an attachment.*'

Q283 **TRUE**. (second paragraph) **A virus can result in the loss of every program and file**. True because '*In a worst case scenario… every program and file will be lost*.'

Q284 **NOT GIVEN**. **Java applets can contain malicious code**. There is no information on Java applets.

Q285 **TRUE**. (fourth paragraph) **A Trojan disguises itself as useful software**. True because '*a trojan is… malware that **masquerades** as useful software*'.

Q286 **FALSE**. (fifth paragraph) **Keystroke logging is always fraudulent**. False because '*Some keystroke loggers operate legitimately.*' Q286 distractor: '*Keystroke logging is the main fraudulent activity linked to spyware.*'

Q287 **FALSE**. (sixth paragraph) **Scareware is not harmful to the user**. False because '*Scareware is a form of extortion where a victim is informed that the computer is infected with a virus, and for a fee…*' The paragraph also indicates that the *user is tricked* and buys software unnecessarily.

Q288   **A.** (second paragraph) <u>a virus</u> **requires user input to infect a computer**. This statement is reflected in the phrase '*A virus can be released when a user*'.

Q289   **C.** (second and third paragraphs) <u>a virus and a worm</u> **can duplicate themselves.** This statement is reflected in '*Viruses can replicate*' (second paragraph) and '*The ability of worms to replicate…*' (third paragraph).

Q290   **B.** (third paragraph) <u>a worm</u> **reduces the computer's speed.** This statement is reflected in '*A main feature of a worm is that it slows the computer down.*'

Q291   **C.** (second paragraph) <u>a virus and a worm</u> **do not damage the hard drive.** This statement is reflected in '*Whilst malware cannot physically damage the computer's hard drive…*' (second paragraph).

Q292   **C.** (seventh paragraph) <u>a virus and a worm</u> **can be removed by security software.** This statement is reflected in '*Security software automatically blocks and **deletes** any malicious programs for a more secure web experience.*'

Reading Passage 11. Highlands and Islands

Q293   **TRUE**. (paragraph A) **The Isles of Lewis and Harris are joined together**. The statement is true **because** '*The Isle of Lewis… a small strip of land connects it to the Isle of Harris, making the two islands one land mass.*'

Q294   **FALSE.** (paragraph A) **There are two islands called Berneray in the sea around Harris**. The statement is false **because**, whilst there are two islands called Berneray, '*The small island of Berneray is connected to North Uist by a causeway and it is the only populated island in the waters around Harris.*'

Q295   **NOT GIVEN. The sea around Benbecula is deep**. There is no information on the depth of the sea around Benbecula. Q295 distractor: 'deeply indented sea lochs' means that the coastline is deeply indented not that the sea is deep.

Q296 **TRUE.** (paragraph B) **On the island of South Uist, there are fertile green grasslands and sandy beaches to the west and many islanders can speak Gaelic**. The statement is true because '*South Uist* is mountainous to the east *with machair and sandy beaches to the west*' and '*machair*' is described earlier as fertile green grassland.

Q297 **FALSE.** (paragraph C) **In the Western Isles most road signs are bilingual**. The statement is false because '*Place names on road signs are in Gaelic with **only the main signs** displaying English beneath.*'

Q298 **TRUE.** (paragraph D) **Approximately 9,000 people live in or near Stornoway**. The statement is true because 'There are approximately *27,000 people* in the Western Isles and *one-third of these live in and around* the capital town of *Stornoway*.

Q299 **FALSE.** (paragraph D) **Most crofters earn their living entirely from crofting**. The statement is false because 'It is difficult to survive from crofting alone and most crofters have to *supplement their incomes with a part-time job.*'

Q300 **A. Lewis**. '*The Isle of Lewis is the most northern and largest…*'

Q301 **D. Eriskay**. '*Eriskay is a tiny island… lying between South Uist and Barra.*'

Q302 **B**. **Berneray**. *Berneray* is connected to *North Uist* by a causeway and it is the only populated island *in the waters around of Harris.* Note that C is Benbecula ('wedged in between' the two Uists) so C cannot be Berneray. Note that the southernmost island is the second Berneray but it is not in the waters around Harris nor is it labelled.

Q303 Paragraph A. **vii) Location.** 'Off the west coast of Scotland, in the Atlantic Ocean, lie a chain of islands known as the Outer Hebrides or Western Isles. Paragraph A talks about the position of the islands in relation to Scotland and the oceans, and goes on to describe the position of the islands in relation to each other.

Q304 Paragraph B. **iv) Landscape.** The paragraph describes the visible features of the land such as the beaches, grasslands and mountains.

Q305 Paragraph C. **ii) Language and culture.** The paragraph begins by saying 'Although part of Scotland, the Western Isles have a distinctive _culture_,' before going on to discuss the use of language on the islands.

Q306 Paragraph D. **v) Population and economic activity.** The passage begins by stating the population of the islands and goes on to discuss industry and 'other areas of economic activity'.

Reading Passage 12. Dummy pills

Q307 **C.** (first paragraph) The passage 'Dummy Pills' is mainly concerned with: **the value and morality of placebo use.** This answer is reflected in 'There is an ongoing debate about the _merits_ and the _ethics_ of using placebos, sometimes called "sugar pills".'

Q308 **B.** (first paragraph) In the passage, the author states that the action of a placebo: **is based on the patient's expectations of success.** This answer is reflected in '_Any benefit that arises from a placebo originates solely in the mind of the person taking it_.' Answer **A**: 'is entirely understood' is untrue ('not completely understood'); answer **C**: 'is based on the active ingredients in the tablet' is untrue ('contains no active ingredients'); answer **D**: 'is entirely psychological' is untrue ('both psychological and physiological').

Q309 **A.** (second paragraph) The author suggests that in volunteers, the placebo effect: **may hide the effect of the drug being tested**. This answer is reflected in 'those who volunteer for a new treatment may show positive health gains from the placebo effect that _masks the response to the treatment_'.

Q310 **D.** (third paragraph) The author states that it is morally wrong for patients to use placebos **instead of their current treatment.** This answer is reflected in '_unethical to stop patients from taking their existing tablets so that they can enter a trial_'.

Q311 **TRUE.** (fourth paragraph) **The author states that quack cures can be likened to complementary and alternative medicine (CAM).** This answer is true **because** '_The modern **equivalent** of these quack cures are "complementary and alternative medicine" (CAM)._'

Q312 **TRUE.** (fourth paragraph) **There are personal accounts of complementary and alternative medicine being successful**. This answer is true **because** 'There is anecdotal evidence from patients that these treatments are effective....'

Q313 **FALSE.** (fourth paragraph) Complementary medicine should be used separately from traditional medicine. This answer is false because '*Complementary therapies are by definition intended to be used alongside traditional medicine as an adjunct treatment.*'

Q314 **TRUE.** (fourth paragraph) **Health improvements following complementary or alternative therapies may not have been caused by the therapies**. This answer is reflected in '*the patient may notice an improvement in their health and link it with the therapy, **when in fact** it is the psychological benefit derived from a bit of pampering in a relaxing environment that has led to feelings of improvement, **or it could be nature taking its course**.*'

Q315 **NOT GIVEN. People turn to complementary and alternative therapies too early.** There is not enough information to say whether this statement is true or false. Q315 distracter: 'Consequently it is important not to turn to alternative therapies too early' (fourth paragraph). Turning too early and not turning are different things.

Q316 **NOT GIVEN.** (fifth paragraph) **There can be risks associated with alternative therapies**. There is no information in the passage on any risks linked with alternative therapies.

Q317 **H. dilemma.** (fifth paragraph) The answer is **dilemma** because '*An ethical dilemma arises when a placebo is considered as a treatment.*' The word *moral* in the question is used in place of the word *ethical* in the passage.

Q318 **A. genuine.** (fifth paragraph) The answer is **genuine** because '*the patient is being deceived into believing that the treatment is authentic*'. The word *tricked* in the question is used in place of the word *deceived* in the passage, and the word *genuine* in the question is used in place of the word *authentic* in the passage.

Q319 **F. harm.** (fifth paragraph) The answer is **harm** because '*that could, if it came to light, jeopardize the relationship between the physician and the patient.*' The words *found out* in the question are used in place of the words *came to light* in the passage and the word *harm* replaces the word *jeopardize*.

Q320   **J. choices.** (fifth paragraph) The answer is **choices** because '*thereby denying patients the right to judge for themselves what is best for their own bodies*' means the same as: patients should not be denied the right to make choices about their own treatment.

Vertical transport

A The raising of water from a well using a bucket suspended from a rope can be traced back to ancient times. (Q358) *If the rope was passed over a pulley wheel it made the lifting less strenuous. The method could be improved upon by attaching an empty bucket to the opposite end of the rope*, then lowering it down the well as the full bucket came up, to counterbalance the weight.

B Some medieval monasteries were perched on the tops of cliffs that could not be readily scaled. To overcome the problem, a basket was lowered to the base of the cliff on the end of a rope coiled round a wooden rod, known as a windlass. It was possible to lift heavy weights with a windlass, especially if a small cog wheel on the cranking handle drove a larger cog wheel on a second rod. (Q348) *Materials and people were hoisted in this fashion* but it was a slow process and if the rope were to break the basket plummeted to the ground.

C In the middle of the nineteenth century the general public considered elevators supported by a rope to be too dangerous for personal use. (Q349) *Without an elevator, the height of a commercial building was limited by the number of steps people could be expected to climb within an economic time period*. It was the American inventor and manufacturer Elisha Graves Otis (1811–61) who finally solved the problem of passenger elevators.

D (Q353) In *1852*, Otis pioneered the idea of a safety brake, and *two years later he demonstrated it* in spectacular fashion at the New York Crystal Palace Exhibition of Industry. Otis stood on the lifting platform, four storeys above an expectant crowd. The rope was cut, and after a small jolt, the platform came to a halt. Otis' stunt increased people's confidence in elevators and sales increased.

E (Q350) The operating principle of the safety elevator was described and *illustrated in its pattern documentation of 1861*. The lifting platform was suspended between two vertical posts each lined with a toothed guide rail. A hook was set into the sides of the platform to engage with the teeth, allowing movement vertically upwards but not downwards. Descent of the elevator was possible only if the hooks were pulled in, which could only happen when the rope was in tension. If the rope were to break, the tension would be lost and the hooks would spring outwards to engage the teeth and stop the fall. Modern elevators incorporate similar safety mechanisms.

F (Q351) Otis installed the first passenger elevator in a store in New York City in *1957*. Following the success of the elevator, taller buildings were constructed, and sales increased once more as the business expanded into Europe. England's first Otis passenger elevator (or lift as the British say) appeared *four years later with the opening of London's Grosvenor Hotel*. Today, the Otis Elevator Company continues to be the world's leading manufacturer of elevators, employing over 60,000 people with markets in 200 countries. More significantly perhaps, the advent of passenger lifts marked the birth of the modern skyscraper.

G Passenger elevators were powered by steam prior to *1902*. A rope carrying the cab was wound round a revolving drum driven by a steam engine. The method was too slow for a tall building, which needed a large drum to hold a long coil of rope. (Q355) *By the following year,* Otis had developed a compact electric traction elevator that used a cable but did away with the winding gear, allowing the passenger cab to be raised over 100 storeys both quickly and efficiently.

H (Q352) *In the electric elevator, the cable was routed from the top of the passenger cab to a pulley wheel at the head of the lift shaft and then back down to a weight acting as a* **counterbalance**. A geared-down electric motor rotated the pulley wheel, which contained a (Q360) groove to *grip* the cable and provide the *traction*. Following the success of the electric elevator, skyscraper buildings began to spring up in the major cities. The Woolworths building in New York, constructed in *1913*, was a significant landmark, being the world's tallest building for *the next 27 years*. It had 57 floors and the Otis high-speed electric elevators could reach the top floor in a little over one minute.

I Each elevator used several cables and pulley wheels, though one cable was enough to support the weight of the car. (Q359) *As a further safety feature*, an oil-filled shock piston was mounted at the base of the lift shaft to act as a buffer, *slowing the car down at a safe rate* in the unlikely event of *every cable failing as well as the safety brake*.

Q348 **FALSE. Only people could be hoisted with a windlass**. The statement is false because 'It was possible to lift heavy weights with a _windlass...._ _Materials and people were hoisted in this fashion._'

Q349 **TRUE. Tall commercial buildings were not economic without an elevator**. The statement is true because '_Without an elevator, the height of a commercial building was limited by the number of steps people could be expected to climb within an economic time period_.'

Q350 **TRUE. Otis' pattern documents contained a diagram.** The statement is true because 'The operating principle of the safety elevator was described and _illustrated_ in its pattern documentation.'

Q351 **FALSE. The first passenger elevator was installed in a hotel**. The statement is false because 'Otis installed the first passenger elevator in a store in New York City in 1957.'

Q352 **TRUE. Electric elevators use similar principles to ancient water-wells**. The statement is true because '_In the electric elevator, the cable was routed from the top of the passenger cab to a pulley wheel at the head of the lift shaft and then back down to a weight acting as a_ **_counterbalance'_**. A similar method of lifting is described in paragraph A where 'The raising of water from a well using a bucket suspended from a rope can be traced back to ancient times. If the _rope was passed over a pulley wheel_ it made the lifting less strenuous. The method could be improved upon by attaching an empty bucket to the opposite end of the rope... to _counterbalance the weight_.'

Q353 **1854.** In what year did Otis demonstrate his safety brake? The answer is found in paragraph D 'In _1852_, Otis pioneered the idea of a safety brake, and two years later he demonstrated it....' (1852 + 2 = 1854)

Q354 **1961.** In what year did the Grosvenor Hotel open in London? The answer is found in paragraph F 'Otis installed the first passenger elevator in a store in New York City in _1957_.' 'England's first Otis passenger elevator... appeared four years later with the opening of London's Grosvenor Hotel.' (1957 + 4 = 1961)

Q355 **1903.** In what year did Otis develop an electric elevator for skyscrapers? The answer is found in passage G 'Passenger elevators were powered by steam prior to _1902_... By the following year, Otis had developed a compact electric traction elevator… allowing the passenger cab to be raised <u>over 100 storeys</u> both quickly and efficiently.' (1902 + 1 = 1903)

Q356   **1941.** In what year was the Woolworths skyscraper no longer the world's tallest building? The answer is found in passage H '<u>The Woolworths building in New York, constructed in *1913*, was a significant landmark, being the world's tallest building for *the next 27 years*</u>. (1913 + 27 = 1940; 1940 is the last year in which it was the tallest; it was no longer the tallest beyond this year, which means by 1941.)

Q357   **Paragraph E.** a method that halts the platform when the rope is cut. The method is described in paragraph **E**. The cutting of the rope is mentioned in paragraph D but not the method by which the platform is brought to a halt.

Q358   **Paragraph A.** two methods that take the strain out of lifting. '<u>If the rope was passed over a pulley wheel *it made the lifting less strenuous*</u>' (first method). *<u>The method could be improved upon by attaching an empty bucket to the opposite end of the rope.…</u>*' (second method).

Q359   **Paragraph I.** a method that prevents injury if all other safety features fail. *<u>As a further safety feature</u>, <u>an oil-filled shock piston was mounted at the base of the lift shaft to act as a buffer, *slowing the car down at a safe rate* in the unlikely event of *every cable failing as well as the safety brake*.</u>*

Q360   **Paragraph H.** a method that applies pressure to a cable to pull it. '<u>a groove to *grip* the cable and provide the *traction*.</u>'

Old dogs and new tricks

Q388   **FALSE.** (first paragraph) Cormorants imprinted on fishermen are difficult to train. The statement is false because '<u>*It is easy to train a cormorant* to behave like this.…</u>'

Q389   **TRUE.** (first paragraph) Imprinting stops young birds from getting separated from their mother. The statement is true because '<u>This "*follow response*" is nature's way of *preventing young birds from straying from their mother*</u>.'

Q390   **TRUE.** (first paragraph) Chicks are sensitive to imprinting for up to 48 hours after hatching. The statement is true because '<u>The process of imprinting lasts for a period *of up to two days* after hatching. After this *sensitive period* the.…</u>'

Q391 **FALSE.** (first paragraph) Imprinting in birds is temporary. The statement is false because 'the effect of the imprinting _remains unchanged for the lifetime_ of the bird and cannot be reversed.'

Q392 **NOT GIVEN. Puppies can only imprint on other dogs and humans**. There is no information in the passage about puppies imprinting on other animal species.

Q393 **D**. (second paragraph) **Socialization of puppies is very important: between the second and fourteenth weeks**, as reflected in '_It is critical that a dog is socialized_ with other dogs, family pets and with people _within this time frame_', meaning the period from the second week to the fourteenth week of life (see Q394a).

Q394 **A**. (second paragraph) **Imprinting in puppies: is complete by the fourteenth week,** as reflected in '_The sensitive period lasts from the second week to the fourteenth week of life_'.

Q395 **B**. (third paragraph) **A puppy that is handled and petted too soon will not: be happy with dogs,** as reflected in 'If a puppy is taken away from its natural mother _too early_ and _handled by people_ then _it sees_ humans as its natural companions and _dogs as complete strangers_.'

Q396 **C**. (fourth paragraph) **Bad behaviour is often: encouraged by mistake,** is reflected in 'Negative behaviours are often _reinforced inadvertently_ when a dog receives more attention for behaving badly than for behaving well.

Q397 **H** (fifth paragraph) by using the toy it likes most (_its favourite toy_).

Q398 **D** (fifth paragraph) using words of approval (_verbally praised_).

Q399 **B** (fifth paragraph) daily training (_training every day_).

Q400 **E** (sixth paragraph) by choosing a suitable breed (_selectively bred_).

Appendix 1

Reading section vocabulary

Reading Passage 1. Shedding light on it

distracter   an incorrect (wrong) answer or statement that attracts the reader's attention.

figure of speech   words with a special meaning that make language more interesting; part of expression; figurative language as distinct from literal language, ie not literally. Examples: to 'burn the midnight oil' is to work late into the night; to 'read between the lines' is to find the hidden message behind what has been written or spoken; requiring 'elbow grease' means needing hard work; shedding light on it – see below.

invisible   not visible

life expectancy   how long something or someone may be expected to live or last

mass production   work performed on production lines

naked eye   unaided eye (without aid, eg without a telescope); a 'figure of speech'

Shedding light on it   'figure of speech': to make clear and understandable

too hot   very hot

traditional   the old way, conventional or accepted way (second meaning: customs and beliefs from earlier times; part of heritage; eg religious practices such as Easter, Christmas, Diwali).

tricked   made to believe something is true when it is not; deceived

Reading Passage 2. Taking soundings

carcases   dead body of an animal
deprives   to be denied something; withheld or taken away
invention   something created that involves a new idea
noise pollution   harmful or unwanted noise
orientate   to turn, steer, or choose a direction
penetrate   to enter into
perception   using the senses to make sense of one's surroundings or situation (eg using your eyes and ears)
phenomenon   an observable fact or event, sometimes a remarkable one
prey   an animal that is hunted
recognize   to identify
reflected back   bounced back
taking soundings   to check out first; assess beforehand ('figure of speech')
vulnerable   at risk of harm

Reading Passage 3. Oxbridge

aspirations   ambitions; what you aspire to or hope to achieve
attainment gap   difference in achievement, eg between boys and girls
derogatory   disrespectful, eg derogatory remarks
expectations   something that you believe will happen in the future
'fit in'   feelings of acceptance or belonging, eg 'fitting in' with the team
gifted   having exceptional ability, eg gifted piano player
link   a connection, relationship or association, eg a link exists between poverty and poor health
merit   deserved, eg awarded top prize based on merit
opportunity   to have been given a chance, eg an opportunity of employment
Oxbridge   a collective term for Oxford and Cambridge Universities
social stratification   refers to social class and inequalities in society
talent   having natural ability and skill, eg a talented and gifted football player
unrealistic   not realistic, not seeing the situation as it really is, eg unrealistic expectations

Reading Passage 4. Rosetta Stone

anniversary   the same date every year (annually) eg wedding anniversary

antiquities   objects from antiquity (earlier or ancient times)

artefacts   man-made object

authentic   genuine, real; not false or copied, not a forgery

context   in a given situation or setting

deciphered   to understand/break a code

declaration   an important statement or announcement

hieroglyphs   words in pictures and symbols

legacy   something handed down from the past; also money left in a will

loan   the act of borrowing something (from a lender) with the intention of returning it, eg to loan the use of a car, or to loan money

lobbied   an attempt to influence a decision

nevertheless   in spite of; however; nevertheless links a previous sentence/idea, eg The IELTS is a difficult test. Nevertheless, most people are successful.

obelisks   tall stone pillar with a pointed top

repatriated   to return someone/something to its place of origin

sacred   something having religious significance

unique   only one, no others; eg a unique web page address

vital   very important; essential.

Reading Passage 5. Tickled pink

benefit   to gain an advantage from; eg recycling benefits the environment

branded   a manufacturer's trademark; often includes a logo, eg McDonald's brand

coarse texture   rough surface

grafted   in horticulture, to insert a bud or shoot into a growing plant

harvesting   the gathering of crops

hue   a colour or range of colours

mutated   a change; in molecular biology, altered DNA sequence of a gene

offspring   a descendant, eg the child of a parent

patent   the legal ownership of an idea or invention to protect it from being copied

phased out   to stop using something gradually

premium   an extra charge or fee

retail   the selling of goods to customers

strains   in biology, different varieties of the same species; eg different varieties of tomatoes (beefsteak, cherry, Cherokee purple); also different breeds of dog

threaten   to express the intention to do harm

tickled pink   'figure of speech', feeling very pleased

tolerance   acceptance of opinions or behaviour that are different from your own

undertone   a colour seen beneath another colour

vigorous   strong and healthy; physical; eg a vigorous plant; a vigorous workout

Reading Passage 6. Bubbly and burgers

barred   prevented

bolster   to strengthen or support

claimant   a person making a claim, eg in a lawsuit; the plaintiff

'copycat'   slang term for copying

deceived   to make something appear true when it is not; to mislead

deemed   considered to be; judged to be

defendant   the person against whom the claim is brought

distinct   different; setting it apart from the rest

distinguish   similar meaning to distinct

emanate   originate

exclusiveness   allowing no others; not sharing

goodwill   the good reputation of the business

invoking   to use a rule or the law

misrepresent   to represent incorrectly

overturned   to reverse a court's decision; also to turn over, tip over

reputation   the character or worth of a person or a business

restricted   limited

usurp   take the place of

Reading Passage 7. Recalling it

apprehensive   fearful

citizen   a member of the public

concurrence   in agreement

cue   reminder; signal

dictaphone   a small cassette recorder for recording and playing back speech

flee   run away; escape from
gesticulations   gestures made with the hand whilst speaking
key elements   important ideas; basic ingredient; eg the key elements of a CV
omitted   missed out
preface   an earlier statement
primitive ancestor   early humans
rambling   a lot of confused or unimportant speech
retrieval   getting back; regaining
rhyme   a small poem that has similar sounding words
salient   important
sequence   in an orderly fashion
stilted   awkward or unnatural in manner
trigger   something that causes a reaction, eg to trigger a memory

Reading Passage 8. Home-schooling

algebra   mathematics where letters are used instead of numbers
ardently   with strong feelings; passionate
compliance   acting as expected to; eg in compliance with the rules and regulations
compulsory   must be done
controversial   causing disagreement or debate
demanding   requiring hard work
detractors   critical; finding fault
dispassionately   without emotional involvement
duty   what you are legally or morally required to do; an obligation
equates   is equal to
equip   to provide with; eg he entered the examination room equipped with the knowledge to achieve a high mark
integrate   to merge together; incorporate
misgivings   feelings of doubt
moral values   accepted ideas about what is right and what is wrong
negate   to make ineffective; nullify
oddity   strange or peculiar
proponents   a person who argues in support of something
pros and cons   arguments for and against (from the Latin 'pro et contra')
rational   reasonable or logical

recreational   activities done for enjoyment, eg sport, games and hobbies
shortcomings   falling short of the expected standard; deficient
socialization   learning the normal behaviour of other people
syllabus   the content of a course of study; the curriculum
unprecedented   not known before

Reading Passage 9. Biofuels backlash

alternatives   other choices
backlash   an opposing reaction
blended   mixed together
brew   alcoholic liquid/beverage; (also slang for a cup of tea)
consumed   taken in and used up (eg consume fuel; consume a meal)
credentials   evidence of suitability or status
deleterious   harmful/negative effect
deplete   to use up
distilling   boiling off (the alcohol)
domestic   home/household
enabling   making it possible for
fermenting   yeast acting on sugar to produce alcohol
fertilizer   nutrients (food) for plants; chemicals/minerals to increase soil fertility
furthermore   in addition to
genuine   being what it is claimed to be; real; authentic; (also truthful)
in theory   according to reasoning or knowledge (in principle) as opposed to 'in
    practice' (in a practical application); eg an engine running on biofuel generates
    less pollution in principle, though in practice it is how it drives that matters
indefinitely   an unlimited period of time
inedible   unsuitable for eating
irrigation   the supply with water
judge   form an opinion; weigh the evidence
leach   to seep out of or drain away
limited   restricted, not endless
mainstay   the main support for
meagre   very small amount; not enough
panacea   a cure/solution for all the problems
particulates   tiny particles (eg soot from a fire)

potent   powerful; having a strong effect
principal   the most important
reap   to get something; also, to gather in
recede   move backwards
reflect   to think carefully
reinforce   strengthen
scrutinize   inspect carefully; examine in detail
spilt   liquid overflowing its container (past participle of the verb 'to spill')
substantial   important; significant
surge   strong forward movement; eg the crowd of people surged forwards
surplus   an excess amount; that which is left over
sustainable   can be maintained

Reading Passage 10. Hacked off

bane   annoyance, causing problems
confidential   private; secret
consequences   caused by something done earlier
criminals   people guilty of crimes
employees   people who do paid work for an employer
extortion   to obtain something, usually money by making threats
fee   money paid out for something; for example, car parking fees
fix   repair/mend; solve
fraudulent   unfair; unlawful; trickery
inadvertently   not intended; a mistake
interfere   to get in the way, meddle with or obstruct
legitimately   legally
malicious   deliberately harmful; with malice
masquerade   pretending to be something or someone that it or she/he is not
metaphor   (part of figurative language) where the words that are normally used (the literal words) are replaced with different words to help to strengthen the message. Examples are: 'A heart of stone' meaning 'to have no feelings; 'It's crystal clear' meaning 'it's well explained'; 'You can't have your cake and eat it' meaning 'you can't have both – you need to choose'
nuisance   annoying; causing bother
scenario   given situation

surreptitiously   done without anyone knowing; quietly

unfettered   free, with no control

victim   a person who is harmed by the actions of someone or something; for example, a victim of crime

Reading Passage 11. Highlands and Islands

causeway   a road or path raised up to cross a stretch of water

chain   follow on from each other

coast   the land near to the sea

decline   reducing in number or amount; a gradual loss

dominant   the most important

dwelling   a home

ferry   a boat or ship that carries people or vehicles across water

hub   at the centre; eg the hub of a wheel

impact   the effect of one thing on another; also a forceful blow or collision

indented   set in from the outside edge

inhabited   live there

leisure time   time spent relaxing rather than working; free time

loch   Gaelic term for a lake or sea inlet (gap where the sea comes in)

naïve   lacking experience and understanding; simplistic

peat   organic material formed when plants partially decay in wetlands

peatland   land made of peat or peat bogs

peculiar   belonging to that one; also unusual or odd

pockmarks   small, hollow depressions; pits

'rat race'   the daily routine or work

reinforces   strengthens

reverse   a complete change in direction; backwards

romanticized   a sentimental view; appealing to the emotions; idealized

Sabbath   day of rest (often a Sunday)

strip   long and narrow

supplement   to add something to make it enough

tradition   customs and beliefs (eg religious practice)

trend   the direction in which something is moving; eg trends in fashion

wedged   a close fit

Reading Passage 12 Dummy pills

50/50 chance   equally likely to occur
adhere   to stick to; to keep with
adjunct   something added on to the main thing
alternative   another choice
apparent   obvious; can be clearly seen
associated   linked or connected with something or someone
authentic   genuine; real
benefit   an advantage or gain
benevolent   charitable; kindly
circumstance   situation; position
complementary   something added to make an improvement; makes complete
debate   a discussion with arguments for and against an issue
deny   to withhold; hold back; also to refuse to admit something
dilemma   a difficult choice to make
dubious   doubtful; not to be relied on
dummy   a copy that looks the same; not the real thing
ethical   moral; according to accepted right and wrong
existing   current; at the time
fake   not genuine; false; a forgery; for example 'a fake driver's licence'
'guinea pig'   person or thing used in an experiment or test
honesty   truthfulness; sincerity
hopes   what you would like to happen in the future
ingredients   the constituents or components of something, especially cookery, as
    in 'the ingredients of bread are flour, margarine, salt, yeast and water'
jeopardize   to put at risk; in harm's way
justified   with good reason; proving to be right
merits   the value or worth of something
ongoing   going on; continuing; not finished
originate   where something begins; stems from
pampering   giving care and attention; eg pampering children, pets, guests, etc
physiological   the biology of the body
pills   medicine tablets
placebo   a pill with no active ingredients; 'sugar pills'
psychological   in the mind; mental state
'quack cure'   a fraudulent remedy with no active or proven ingredients

random   in no particular order; no pattern

remedies   a medicine to relieve pain or cure something; for example 'cough and cold remedies'

solely   on its own; no other; the only one

therapeutic   health benefits; healing; therapy

treatment   medical care; it also means the way of dealing with something or someone, as in 'minority groups not receiving fair treatment'

unproven   not proven; not shown to be true

volunteer   unpaid worker

Vertical Transport

advent   the coming of something important, eg the advent of electric lighting

buffer   something that reduces the shock of impact; bumper

cog wheel   wheel with teeth

coiled   wound in a loop

compact   taking little space

counterbalance   a balancing weight

drum   a cylinder to take the winding; also, a container or a percussion instrument

engage   connect with; lock into

groove   a narrow cut; channel

illustrated   shown by way of a diagram or picture

incorporate   to include

landmark   a feature of the landscape that stands out

medieval   the 'middle ages'; period in history from around 500AD to 1500AD

monasteries   houses for monks (people who have taken religious vows)

piston   a solid cylinder that fits tightly inside a hollow cylinder

plummeted   to descend or drop rapidly

revolving   rotating; spinning; eg revolving door

rope   a thick, braided line or cord

scaled   climbed

significantly   importantly

spectacular   something dramatic or sensational

strenuous   hard work

stunt   something done to attract publicity or attention

suspended   hang from; dangle

Old dogs and new tricks

'You can't teach an old dog new tricks' (proverb) means it's difficult to get people to change their old ways of doing something (old habits) or to learn something new.

ability   being able to do something

adequate   enough; sufficient

aggressive   likely to start a fight or attack; hostile

associate   links or connects

captivity   held without freedom; imprisoned

cliché   a tired or overused idea or statement

cling   to hold on tightly

companion   a friend or animal that travels with you

comply   to be obedient

conversely   in the opposite way

dangerous   likely to do harm or cause injury

deliberate   done with intention and purpose; not by mistake

domesticated   tamed (controlled) eg as a pet

enhanced   to improve something or encourage it

favourite   something you like the most; eg favourite TV show

inadvertently   by mistake

obedience   doing what you are told to do

praise   use words of approval such as 'well done', 'good dog'

retrieve   bring back; fetch

selectively bred   choosing which animals (or plants) should mate to produce desirable qualities

socialize   mix with others in a group

stranger   someone who is not known; unfamiliar

stray   to move away/wander away and risk becoming lost

suit   suitable; fits with

suppressed   to hold back or prevent something

track   follow

traditional   the old way, conventional or accepted way (second meaning: customs and beliefs from earlier times; part of heritage; eg religious practices such as Easter, Christmas, Diwali)

verbally   with speech

Appendix 2

British and American spellings

You can use British or American spellings in the IELTS without being penalized but you should be consistent. For example: flavours and colours ✓ (British); flavors and colors ✓ (American); flavours and colors ✗ (British and American). Selected spellings are listed below.

British	American
advertise	advertize
aluminium	aluminum
axe	ax
brunette	brunet
centre	center
cheque	(pay)check
colour	color
co-operate	cooperate
defence	defense
disc	disk
enrol	enroll

British	American
flavour	flavor
grey	gray
humour	humor
install	instal
judgement	judgment
kilometre	kilometer
labour	labor
litre	liter
memorise	memorize
metre	meter
neighbour	neighbor
offence	offense
programme	program
pyjamas	pajamas
rumour	rumor
summarise	summarize
travelled	traveled
tyre	tire
utilise	utilize
vapour	vapor
wilful	willfull
yoghurt	yogurt